Well Blow Me Down

DISCARD

Well Blow Me Down

A Guy's Guide to Talking Like a Pirate

The indispensable aid to getting the most out of Talk Like a Pirate Day

By John Baur and Mark Summers
Co-creators of the new international holiday, Talk Like a Pirate Day, celebrated every September 19th

Printed in the United States of America.

Published by The Pirate Guys, LLC
840 Broadway S.W.
Albany OR 97321
www.talklikeapirate.com

The Pirate Guys, LLC, is represented by Scott Hoffman,
PMA Literary & Film Management, Inc.
45 W. 21st Street
Sixth Floor,
New York, NY 10038
212-929-1222 (v) 212-206-0238 (f)
www.pmalitfilm.com

ISBN: 1-59571-022-1
Library of Congress Control Number: 2004107959

Word Association Publishers
205 5th Avenue,
Tarentum, PA 15084
www.wordassociation.com

Table of Contents

Introduction,
plundered from Dave Barry

The following is taken with permission from the writing of syndicated columnist Dave Barry, winner of the Pulitzer Prize and our close personal friend, although in the name of complete candor we have to admit that we've never actually met the man.

September 8th, 2002

Every now and then, some visionary individuals come along with a concept that is so original and so revolutionary that your immediate reaction is: "Those individuals should be on medication."

Today I want to tell you about two such people, John Baur and Mark Summers, who have come up with a concept that is going to make you kick yourself for not thinking of it first: Talk Like a Pirate Day. As the name suggests, this is a day on which everybody would talk like a pirate. Is that a great idea, or what? There are so many practical benefits that I can't even begin to list them all.

Baur and Summers came up with this idea a few years ago.

They were playing racquetball, and, as so often happens, they began talking like pirates. And then it struck them: Why not have a day when EVERYBODY talks like a pirate? They decided that the logical day would be September 19th, because that – as you are no doubt aware – is Summers' ex-wife's birthday.

Since then, Baur and Summers have made a near-superhuman effort to promote Talk Like a Pirate Day. As Baur puts it: "We've talked like pirates, and encouraged our several friends to, every September 19th, except for a couple where we forgot."

And yet, incredibly, despite this well-orchestrated campaign, the nation has turned a deaf shoulder to Talk Like a Pirate Day. In desperation, Baur and Summers turned to me for help ... So I have decided to throw my full support behind Talk Like a Pirate Day ...

Talking like a pirate will infuse your everyday conversations with romance and danger. So join the movement! On September 19th, do not answer the phone with "hello." Answer the phone with "Ahoy me hearty!" If the caller objects that he is not a hearty, inform him that he is a scurvy dog (or, if the caller is female, a scurvy female dog) who will be walking the plank off the poop deck and winding up in Davy Jones' locker, sleeping with the fishes. No, wait, that would be Talk Like a Pirate in "The Godfather" Day ...

But the point is, this is a great idea, and you, me bucko, should be part of it. Join us on September 19th You HAVE the buckles, darn it: Don't be afraid to swash them! Let's make this into a grass-roots movement that sweeps the nation, like campaign-finance reform, or Krispy Kreme doughnuts. I truly think this idea could bring us, as a nation, closer together.

But not TOO much closer. Some of us will have swords.

Chapter 1
Meet the Pirate Guys

Arrr! We be two guys, matey. Or, if you prefer, we are two guys, John Baur and Mark Summers. We suppose, by definition, by biology, by whatever, we are men. But we usually think of ourselves as guys, and that's probably all you need to know to understand what follows.

Dave Barry, the great chronicler of guy lore, not to mention a Pulitzer Prize-winning humor columnist and our close personal friend (although we've never actually been in the same Zip code as him) explains this distinction as well as it can be explained in his book, *Dave Barry's Complete Guide To Guys*. So if you are still standing in the bookstore flipping through this volume trying to decide whether to buy it (and remember, a bookstore isn't a library – fork over the cash and take this book home) you might want to see if they also have that excellent book. We owe it to Dave to help him sell a couple of extra books, because he helped get us started, though he may not want the credit. But buy our book, too. Or, if you're only going to buy one, then we've gotta say, go with ours. Dave is on his own.

But the point here is, we are guys. And guys, as most women will tell you, are apt to do just the stupidest things. Which is how Talk Like a Pirate Day first got started, then grew to a national and then international phenomenon. And we don't use those words lightly, although we're not sure we spelled them right.

Our little idea was born on a racquetball court as we flailed ineffectually at a bouncing blue ball and hurled insults at each other in pirate lingo. Why? It's hard to say. Maybe one of us strained a muscle while reaching for a shot and cried out, "Aarrr!" and the rest just followed. It could have happened that way. We decided right then and there that the world needed a holiday where everyone talked like a pirate. We settled on September 19th because it is Mark's ex-wife's birthday. The day was stuck in his head and he wasn't doing anything with it anymore.

From such unlikely beginnings, Talk Like a Pirate Day has taken on a worldwide life of its own. The whole country got caught up in the talk-like-a-pirate fervor. The whole world. We've been on CNN, the BBC, and in newspapers and on radio stations around the world.

Men and women around the globe have clasped this idea to their bosoms, figuratively speaking, and made it their own. And we found ourselves thinking, "We have performed a national service. We have created an outlet by which guys can express themselves in an unapologetically manly way, all the while enhancing their communication with other guys. This is our contribution to world peace. We are benefactors to the entire human race!

"So how do we make a buck off this?"

The answer, of course, is this book.

Chapter 2

Why is this day different from all other days?

Every September 19th, it's time to celebrate the newest worldwide holiday by talking like a pirate.

The first question is: why? The how we can deal with later, but the first question everyone asks is: Why do we need International Talk Like a Pirate Day? OK, actually that's the second question. The first is: Are you guys nuts? The answer is yes. Then they ask the second question.

Make no mistake. We need such a day. But it's a little hard to articulate why, especially to your wife when you've made the mistake of referring to her as a scurvy bilge rat and tried to order her back into the galley. (See the section on "Talking Like a Pirate Around the House." In fact, most guys should probably just skip ahead to that section first for valuable advice, then come back here and pick this up at your leisure. Go ahead. We'll wait ... OK, let's continue.)

Talking like a pirate is fun. It's really that simple. It gives your conversation a swagger, an élan, denied to landlocked lubbers like yourself (and there's LOTS more to say about lubbers, as you'll be surprised to learn.) The best explanation came from a guy at a Cleveland radio station who interviewed us on the 2002 Talk Like a Pirate Day. By then the day had turned from a small, private joke into an international event and we were fairly flummoxed (not a pirate word, that we know of, but a pretty good one, you'll admit.) He told us we were going to be inundated by people asking for interviews because it was a "whimsical alternative" to all the serious things that were making the news so depressing. In other words, its silliness is its best selling point.

What's the point?

So what is it exactly that we're celebrating here, if not pirates? What, you're wondering, is the point?

We're going to be painfully honest here, perhaps fatally so. The point is there is no point. And that's what's fun about talking like a pirate in general and the idea of having an international holiday when everyone does it. We're talking about the mere image of swaggering pirateness. It's one day a year when you can be unapologetically who you really are or, perhaps more to the point, who you envision yourself to be. For one day, be Errol Flynn. Or at least Johnny Depp.

And while this is a guys' guide, the comely wench will have fun talking like a pirate, too. That's been another surprise, one that we have to say we enjoyed. Women, at least the boisterous, fun-loving yet still wildly attractive types, have been getting into the holiday as well. Lots of them.

It's powerful, yet harmless. Perhaps, dare we suggest it, the ultimate aphrodisiac. Try it!

Chapter 3
It's all about Pirattitude

The heart of International Talk Like a Pirate Day is not in nautical words or phrases offered up with a thick Cornish accent. You won't find it in severed limbs, wooden peg legs and black eye-patches. It won't even be found in the paper pirate hats worn by investment bankers in boardrooms around the world or in the muffled screams of third-graders when their teacher brandishes a papier-mâché belaying pin and threatens to keelhaul their tiny pirate booties. Although both of these things have happened on the last couple of September 19ths. We have the photos to prove it.

Nay, the heart of International Talk Like a Pirate Day is in what we like to call "Pirattitude."

Pirattitude, like the concept of attitude or the definition of pornography, may not be easy to define, but you know it when you see it. To truly understand your own level of Pirattitude, we need to take a walk into the dark recesses of your imagination. We have devised a brief, "finish the story" scenario for you. We will assess your answer and tell you whether or not you have true Pirattitude.

Marvin was walking home from work on a sunny Wednesday afternoon. The day had been uneventful, relatively speaking. He had been called into the boss's office to talk about his job performance. "Marvin," the boss began, "I think we need to discuss your paperwork. You're two months behind and we here at -" Suddenly Marvin:

(a) begins weeping, apologizing and begging the boss not to fire him.

(b) leans back, lights a cigar and says, "You can have genius or you can have paperwork. You can't have both. Now, get out of my office and get to work."

If you answered (b) you may well be on your way to claiming Pirattitude. If you answered (a), we have some work to do. Let's start by recognizing that there is a freedom in being completely screwed. Your pay stinks. Your job stinks. You suspect your spouse is cheating on you. Your children laugh at you, and not even behind your back. Each month places you deeper in debt, and the only glimmer of hope in your pitiful life is that the same month that makes you poorer also brings you thirty days closer to the merciful release of inevitable death. See? You are completely screwed. You have nothing to lose. Your boss won't be expecting it when you go back and choose (b.) Remember: He can kill you, but he can't eat you. That's against the rules. Now, let's pick up the story:

Marvin's stunned boss gets up, collects his few personal belongings and begins to leave. "Where will I work now?" A kindly, generous smile crosses Marvin's face. "Oh, by all means, take my old cubicle." "Thank you," the boss says as he stumbles out the door. Marvin puts his feet on the desk and breathes in the cigar smoke. Soon the phone rings. It's the chief financial officer. She is gorgeous but has a reputation for crushing the testicles – real and metaphorical – of all the male managers and even some board members when she finds them weak and tedious. She says, "I want you in my office ten minutes ago, where the hell are you?" Marvin takes another drag off the cigar, then he:

(a) explains that he is new and didn't get the memo. He asks if she can hold on another five minutes while he gathers some papers.

(b) tells her the only meeting he will be attending is the one where she comes to HIS office in her best "kitten with a whip" costume and begs him to be "gentle with your little minx, Guvnuh!" "Aye," Marvin adds, "ye be a saucy wench!"

If you answered (b) yet again, you seem to have been channelling Pirattitude from somewhere. Are you related to Clark Gable or Douglas Fairbanks? Unfortunately, our friends who answered (a) will need to see a doctor and have a Pire-x-ray to see if there is any hope of some therapeutic intervention stimulating their pirate gene.

Let's take one last run at our story, shall we?

On the walk home, Marvin wonders what kind of car he will buy with his new position, increased income and feverishly hot, rich new girlfriend. Suddenly, the neighbor's rabid mastiff, Adolf, charges the distracted man from behind. At a distance of about six feet, the dog releases a blood-curdling "WOOF" and is about to leap toward Marvin's unprotected neck. At this exact moment, Marvin:

(a) loses control of his bladder and freezes motionless on the sidewalk as the huge, enraged dog sinks his shark-like teeth into the back of Marvin's neck, crushing his spinal cord and sending Marvin's body to the sidewalk where he breathes out his last.

(b) wheels around toward the leaping, snarling nightmare of death and delivers a crushing head butt directly between the airborne canine's eyes. The dog lands in a heap on the sidewalk and rolls about yelping and trying to recover his footing. Marvin stands, fists clinched, arms akimbo, awaiting the second wave of an attack that never comes. Passers-by later tell of a deep, resonant growl emitting from the scene which they first attributed to the hound, until they discovered the sound persisted even after the beast had turned tail and run for the safety of an oncoming train.

Alright. If you selected (a) again, you not only have no hope of ever achieving Pirattitude but clearly cannot distinguish a pattern of behavior and therefore cannot be trusted with any of your own life choices. Of course (b) is the right choice. Who chooses dying on a sidewalk of a dog-inflicted spinal cord injury over classic victory complete with war-growling and standing arms akimbo? We're talking ARMS AKIMBO here, people!

Let's hope that this brief lesson and overview of Pirattitude not only taught you valuable dog-fighting skills, but inspired you to take more pride in your work ... and to do your paperwork in a timelier manner.

Your authors are so overcome with Pirattitude that we've even given ourselves pirate names. Not fierce, evil pirate names like Black Death Baur or Mad Mark the Shipburner. No, while we sometimes wish we had done so (purely for wenching reasons,) we gave ourselves somewhat whimsical pirate names. Because we need to remind ourselves, and through this book and our Web site you as well, that there is more than a little whimsy in the whole idea of trying to get everybody on the planet to talk like a pirate every September 19th.

Mark went with Cap'n Slappy as his nom de pirate, envisioning the cap'n as a blustery, benevolent but ultimately fierce pirate chieftain – at least, fierce in the wenching and drinking categories. The stories over how he got the peg leg, the patch and the hook change so often we're never sure what to believe. John went with the name Ol' Chumbucket. (You'll learn what that means later in this book; it's not a compliment.) John sees Ol' Chumbucket as a mysterious figure of undetermined rank, Cap'n Slappy's best drinking buddy, and a failed ship's cook. He was given the name by a crew unappreciative of his limited culinary skills. John's children would be happy to provide testimonials to that fact.

If you can balance the fierceness with the sense of whimsy, and let it be known that you really don't care what the world thinks of you – you're harming no one, but no one is going to harm you either – then you have it. You've got Pirattitude, matey!

Chapter 4

A quick quiz

And now, just for fun, a little pirate trivia quiz. Some of this stuff is so easy you won't believe we're even asking. And some of it you will learn later in the book anyway, so we'll ask you now so that we can look smart, if only for a few more pages.

And even if any of these questions seem obscure or difficult, the wrong answers tend to be so obviously wrong that you couldn't possibly miss them. But if you don't want to take the quiz, don't bother. There's nothing riding on it, and a big part of Pirattitude is doing what you want and to hell with everybody else. If that's the kind of guy you are, flip ahead to the next chapter. But we think you'll enjoy it, so we urge you to read on.

Here's Cap'n Slappy's little quizzie. And if you like his little quizzies, wait till you see his little testies.

Remember, this is for entertainment only: No wagering, please.

1. Blackbeard the Pirate's REAL name was.
   a) Lemming Bolderduck
   b) Ralph Stonecrusher
   c) Sven Takahashi
   d) Edward Teach

2. Blackbeard's ship was called The _____
   a) Sissybritches
   b) Queen's Potty
   c) Queen Anne's Revenge
   d Gropenator

3. During a battle, Blackbeard would _____
   a) dress up like a nurse.
   b) tie and light burning wicks in his hair and beard
   c) threaten to spank anyone who didn't fight fair.
   d) sing dirty Irish limericks at the top of his lungs.

4. A "privateer" is a pirate who _____
   a) works under the protection of a government
   b) wears blue velvet britches
   c) plays the concertina
   d) pretends he is going to shake hands with someone then suddenly pulls away.

5. The most successful pirate in history was _____
   a) a circus clown who invented the "honk-honk" horn.
   b) Ching Yih Saoa, a Chinese woman who inherited the pirate business from her husband and built it into a fleet of more than 800 junks.
   c) an Australian cross-dresser who called himself "The Marquis D'Saucypants"
   d) a badger named "Rascal."

6. Before a battle, a smart, well-trained pirate might spread _____ on the decks.
   a) a little love
   b) sand
   c) a thin coating of tar and urine
   d) the contents of the nearest chumbucket

7. A pirate flag is referred to as _____
   a) a Jolly Roger
   b) a Jolly Manfred
   c) a Bloody Bobby
   d) Me Ol' Snot-catcher

8. Grog is the standard drink aboard a pirate ship and it consists of:
   a) vodka, Frangelico, Irish Cream and Sprite
   b) beer and whiskey.
   c) rum, coconut milk and a splash of lime
   d) rum and water

9. Pirates are well known to accessorize their ensemble – for instance, pirates wore a large gold earring to _____

   a) let other pirates know that they fancied a bit o' the "bouncy-bouncy" and weren't too particular as to their "bouncy" partner.
   b) cover the cost of their funeral which, in their line of work, seemed to be a well-thought-out retirement plan.
   c) signify that, "I've plundered all over the world, and all I could get meself was this blasted earring!"
   d) symbolize the "One-ness of being in the circle of life" that could only be found in a life characterized by brutality and greed.

10. Talk Like a Pirate Day is celebrated on September 19th because it is:
   a) Blackbeard's birthday.
   b) Cap'n Slappy's ex-wife's birthday.
   c) the night they invented champagne.
   d) the day the musical Pirates of Penzance debuted in London

The correct (more or less) answers: 1 - d, 2 - c; 3 - b; 4 - a; 5 - b; 6 - b; 7 - a; 8 - d; 9 - b; 10 - b.

Chapter 5

Pirate Talk, a glossary

So here you are, at the heart of the book, the reason, presumably, that you bought this tome in the first place or that someone bought it for you (and if that's the case, lucky you. You have good friends.) In the next few pages, you will learn all anyone could need to know about how to talk like a pirate. And if you pick up the lingo, we are confident that you'll pick up the Pirattitude.

Before we start breaking down the lingo for you, we need to be clear about which pirates we're trying to talk like, because piracy is as old as sailing. We would guess that the first boat was invented by a guy who wanted to get somewhere by water, the second by his friend, who wanted to race him and show how much better he was, and the third by someone who wanted to rob both of the first two while they were off drinking beer. The word "pirate" itself comes from the ancient Greek word peiren, which means "assault."

What follows will not be a list of phrases in Greek. Or Spanish, French, Chinese, or anything other than English, even though there were pirates of these nationalities and probably all the rest. We speak English, and the pirate movies we grew up with were all in English. We are talking here about the classic, popular image of a pirate as embodied in the kinds of movies, books and TV shows we grew up with – the buccaneers of the 17th through the mid-19th century, plundering Spanish shipping from the New World and burying their treasure on remote islands.

If we have left out your favorite phrase, we apologize, but we've been as complete as we can be without doing a lot of actual work. And we don't mean to exclude other pirates from other times and parts of the world. We just don't know much about them. The point of the holiday and this book is to have fun. If you believe we have made a mistake in one of our definitions, we're perfectly willing to concede the point, as long as you're willing to concede that we really don't care. Our research involved more beer and pizza than actually looking things up.

Still, we have been forced, almost against our will, to actually learn things. People have read some of our comments on the Web and written in to set us straight. Lubber, for instance, and swashbuckler were a couple of terms that we used carelessly and got an earful over. And so we try to be accurate when we can, but we just want you to understand that accuracy wasn't even close to our first priority.

So, with that said, let's dive into pirate lingo and lore.

Exclamations

We begin with these five entries because they are the cement that binds together pirate lingo. Even if you don't know a foc's'le from a reef or a glory hole from a broadside, you can still give your conversation a pirate-like panache by injecting a fair number of these exclamations into the mix.

Avast – Stop and give attention. It can be used in a sense of surprise, "Whoa! Get a load of that!" when a beautiful woman walks into the room. "Avast! Check out the bowsprit on that fine beauty!" you might say.

Ahoy – "Hello!"

Aye – "Why, yes, I agree most heartily with everything you just said or did."

Aye aye – "I'll get right on that, sir, as soon as my break is over." It suddenly occurs to us that we've never heard any similarly colorful expressions for "no," perhaps because pirates were the type you didn't want to say no to.

And then there's this tricky one:

Arr – This one is often confused with arrgh, which is of course the sound you make when you sit on a belaying pin. "Arr!" can mean, variously, "yes," "I agree," "I'm happy," "I'm enjoying this beer," "My team is going to win it all," "I saw that television show, it sucked," "I am here and alive" and "That was a clever remark you or I just made." And those are just a few of the myriad possibilities of "Arrr!" It's a little bit like the pirate version of "Oy," that indispensable Yiddish word that has almost as many meanings as there are ways to pronounce it. To give the proper "Arr," start by standing with your feet apart, about shoulder width. Arms akimbo (this means with your fists planted on your hips, elbows wide. If we ever decide to become professional wrestlers, we think Arms Akimbo would be a GREAT wrasslin' name.) Then start a rumble in your belly and, with all the Pirattitude you can muster, let it rise up your throat and burst out gutturally – "Aaaarrrr!" You've got it!

Just sprinkle a few ayes, arrs and avasts into your conversation (and maybe one or two oys, if you want to be a Jewish pirate) and you're more than halfway to being safe in port.

The rest of pirate argot can be divided roughly into three sections: Things you could call a person or that a person could be, things that are things, and things you can do with the other things. This is a very subjective classification system, and some of these entries could appear in more than one category. But we had to start somewhere.

We would add one warning here. Reading through this is likely to impart some actual knowledge. We can't help it. If you want to learn how to use these words, you probably should know what they mean, and sometimes we actually knew, unlikely though that seems. Sometimes there are some interesting things to learn (see, for instance, the heading for "pieces of eight.") But it is not our main intention to be teachers or anything, even though we have both worked at schools. Nor do we claim to be perfect. This is a pirate's lexicon as spoken in a 21st century sports bar. We tried to be correct. We've had people pass dozens of words and phrases on to us, and we've checked them as best we could without actually working too hard. But when offered a choice between two definitions, we went with the more entertaining one every time.

Things a person could be

Barnacle – This is a family of crustaceans that form a hard shell and attach themselves to rocks and the hulls of ships. Left to themselves they can cause significant damage to the bottom of a wooden ship, and so must be scraped off periodically. In pirate lingo, calling a person a barnacle is, if not quite a compliment, at least a sign of respect, or even manly affection. "You old barnacle," you might say, lauding him for his crustiness.

Beauty – The best possible pirate address for a woman. Always preceded by "me," as in, "C'mere, me beauty," or even "me buxom beauty," to one particularly well-endowed. Guys will be surprised how effective this is. In fact, it was this line that first woke us to the universal appeal of Talk Like a Pirate Day, when John's wife, Tori, responded favorably. "Does this mean you have to call me, 'me beauty'?" she asked. Indeed it does.

Bilge rat – The bilge is the lowest level of the ship. It's loaded with ballast, which is a heavy weight (usually rocks) that keeps the ship from tipping over at sea, and slimy, reeking water. A bilge rat, then, is a rat that lives in the bilge of the ship. A lot of guy humor involves insulting your buddies to prove your friendship. It's important that everyone understand you are smarter, more powerful and much luckier with the wenches than they are. Since "bilge rat" is a pretty dirty thing to call someone, by all means use it on your friends.

Boarders – Pretty much every pirate movie has a scene in which the pirates, with knives clenched in their teeth, swarm across the railing from their ship or swing from the rigging onto the deck of their opponents' vessel. They are boarders. When you swing into a bar or a party at someone's house, you could be one too. Be sure to call out, "Boarders away," or something similar as you make your entrance.

Bloody – This actually is quite offensive in some English-speaking countries. Seems silly, what with all the profanities that permeate our language today, but there you go. Bloody is an adjective indicating disapproval. "The bloody copy machine is jammed again," you might say. "When the repairman gets here, he's walkin' the plank!"

Bosun – A shortened form of boatswain, a ship's petty officer, midway in rank between the commissioned officers and the crew. There's nothing petty about a petty officer. Almost any old salt will tell you that it's really the petty officers who run the ship.

Brethren of the Coast – A name the pirates of the Caribbean gave themselves. They actually formed a loose association, and never (or at least rarely) attacked or stole from each other. That is, not until about 1680, when a new generation of pirates appeared with less regard for the "old ways" and more interest in stealing a buck wherever they could find one. It's the same old story every time, isn't it? These new kids with their newfangled ways. This seems as good a place as any to mention that the buccaneer communities of the Caribbean were often homosexual, and point out the reality that aboard a crowded ship full of blackguards and men for whom law and custom meant little, the incidence of homosexual acts (in the absence of much female company) was probably pretty high. Not that there's anything wrong with that. We just thought we ought to mention that in fairness. So perhaps if a group of gay friends wanted to celebrate Talk Like a Pirate Day, they could bill themselves as "the Brethren of the Coast."

Buccaneer – From a French word, boucanier, literally meaning "one who hunts wild pork." It comes from a specific way of cooking wild pork and cattle found in the Caribbean. It's kind of a long story, and while it has the ring of truth, we can't verify it. It's just one of those things we heard. But here goes. The Spanish wanted the Western Hemisphere to themselves. (Yes, there were already people living here.

Complain to the Spanish, not us.) The Spanish had a tendency to kill any non-Spanish colonists they found in the New World. Groups of settlers in the Caribbean, first French and then Dutch, English and others, lived in isolation and subsisted mostly on wild pigs that lived on the islands. They became really good at catching them and killing them with knives, rarely having to resort to shooting them. The meat was cut into strips and laid on a grating of green wood called a barbecu (hence our word barbecue) above a slow-burning fire, and was cured by the heat and smoke. The cured meat was called "boucan." The Spanish left them alone for a while, but eventually decided they constituted a menace that had to be driven out. They tried killing off the wild game by which the boucaniers - now buccaneers - lived. When that didn't work, they turned to actually trying to kill off the buccaneers, who took it personally. This made the latter easily recruited by the English for raiding the Spaniards. The early buccaneers did not often attack English shipping. On the whole they found a broader and more profitable lifestyle on the open seas preying on Spanish treasure ships than they had chasing pigs on the islands. This is why every September 19th, you want to celebrate the holiday with a plate of barbecued pork ribs. We certainly do.

Bucko – Friend, mate, buddy. Homey, if you will. Like so many pirate pleasantries and endearments, works well with a possessive "me" in front, such as, "Well done, me bucko," when your friend brings a round of drinks. It is taken, not, as you might expect, from "buccaneer," but from "buck," a male deer.

Cap'n – This is a title of respect, the rank of a person who commands a ship. Do not confuse it with skipper, which has an unfortunate connotation. (See "Skipper," below.) We would just note that, in our experience, on Talk Like a Pirate Day, almost everyone calls him or her self Cap'n this, that or the other thing. Certainly we can't ALL be captains, can we? We've gotta have a crew. Now, it is a fact that pirate ships typically were democratic, in that the crew elected its captain and officers. And that's how we'd advise settling things. When you get together with your crew on September 19th, why not hold a vote to see who gets to be called captain? It could be fun, and will give the unsuccessful candidates something to brood over for the next year.

Corsair – Another name for pirate, more often, we think, applied to the pirates of the Barbary Coast of "Shores of Tripoli" fame than the classic Caribbean pirate, but still, a pirate all the same.

Freebooter – Yet another word for pirate.

Lubber – A lubber is an incompetent sailor or oaf, or someone who does not go to sea, who stays on the land. One is tempted to guess that the word comes from a slurring of "land lover," although that's only a guess. As it turns out, the guess is wrong, as we were told at great length after using the phrase on our Web site. One correspondent went so deeply into the derivation of the word (he seemed to think it was Danish or Dutch or something) that, quite frankly, our eyes glazed over. The guy was probably right, but he also apparently was NOT the sort of person you would take on a long sea voyage. WE'RE KIDDING, of course. Not only do we LIKE it when people tell us we're wrong, we actually enjoy being talked into a coma. Anyway, our dictionary seems to indicate it's from Middle English, but there's no way we're going to print that, because it will engender another long letter that we frankly don't have the strength to read.

The word "lubber" is one of the more fierce weapons in

your arsenal of pirate lingo. In a room where everyone is talking like pirates, lubber is ALWAYS an insult.

Laddie – Ostensibly a term of affection, with a touch of paternalism ("Aye, you're a good laddie") but because it's a diminutive, it's actually a bit of a slam. It's a backhanded way to point out that you're more mature, wise, manly and successful with women than your friend could ever hope to be. So use it often.

Lassie – A diminutive for girl, woman or sweetheart. Don't use it in addressing a woman and then make the obvious pun about the famous movie dog. Not if you want to get any that night.

Matey – A shipmate, a friend or buddy. When people live in as close proximity as pirates do, sharing sleeping quarters and pillaging and never doing laundry, mateys can be very close friends indeed.

Me – Replaces "my" in all uses, such as "Come here, me beauty," or, "Wait'll you taste me cutlass." Use it to indicate possession. DO NOT use it to replace "I" for the first-person singular, as in, "Me was thinkin' of ..." Save that for Talk Like a Caveman Day.

Salt or salty – A salt is someone who is wise to the ways of the sea. The sea is, of course, salt water, so a person long exposed to it is ... salty. Salty language, of course, tends to be coarse, but hey, so is unrefined salt.

Sea dog – A seasoned, hardened, hard-core sailor, one who has looked on storm and gale and braved the worst the sea can offer. Francis Drake was a sea dog.

Seaworthy – Capable of handling the sea and all its dangers. Is there a finer compliment from one nautical person to another? We thought not.

Shark bait – A person who's been thrown overboard without benefit of a life jacket, because they will presumably be eaten by sharks. In point of fact, sharks rarely attack people. You'd be far more likely to drown, which in the end probably isn't any more fun but is far more accurate. But in the lingo, accuracy is often tossed overboard in the name of being colorful, so "shark bait" it is.

Skipper Technically, this means the same thing as cap'n, but it currently has a mocking connotation. This generation will have to pass away before the word is free of the taint brought on by its use as the name of a character on "Gilligan's Island." (Although we have to admit a grudging admiration for actor Alan Hale Jr., who played the Skipper, and even more for his dad, also an actor. Is it just us, or were that father and son virtually indistinguishable, even down to their acting styles?) Needless to say, "little buddy" is not even a little piratical.

Swashbuckler – One who engages in showy heroics. The all-time great swashbuckler was Errol Flynn, the star of "The Seahawk" and "Captain Blood," two of the best pirate movies ever made (and who made a couple of movies with Alan Hale Sr.). The true swashbuckler performs his dangerous deeds with a brio and savoir-faire that makes the risk of his life seem a matter of no consequence. It's all a question of style. It has been pointed out to us by the persnickety that you can swash your buckle, but you cannot buckle your swash. The latter phrase makes no sense at all. Why? Because your buckle is a shield (isn't "sword and buckler" a Biblical phrase? We should probably know that). And swashing it means clashing it in a loudly fierce way to frighten the enemy before engaging him or her in combat. And that's more than we ever wanted to know about the subject.

Wench – A saucy woman, typically of a lower class – barmaids, actresses, that sort of thing. It used to mean a young woman, plain and simple. But try explaining that to the woman who works in the next cubicle when she takes offense at your use of the word. The word "wench" works best with "spicy" tasting modifiers, including the word spicy itself. Think about it – "spicy wench," "saucy wench," "sweet wench," "tart wench."

Ye – An archaic form of "you." We've seen people seriously overuse this one. A little ye goes a long way, so use it sparingly or ye might live to regret it.

Things that are things

Aft – Short for "after," it refers specifically to the rear of the ship, and more generally can be used to refer to the rear of anything or anyone. A pirate describing overtaking a prey might say something like, "She tried to turn tail, but we took her from the aft and boarded." It has a much different connotation today, doesn't it?

Ale – The nectar of the guys. The delicious, frothy mixture of water, grain, hops and yeast, it is the beverage that does much to justify God's ways to man, or at least explain man's ways to God.

Belaying pin – Did you ever watch a pirate movie and notice that in hand-to-hand conflict, they were often swinging these short wooden clubs at each other? They (the clubs, not the pirates) seem to be posted all over the railings of the ship, and are the perfect objects for sneaking up behind someone and whacking them in the head with. But where did they come from? What are they? For years we wondered, "Why do these ships keep racks full of cudgels along the railing, providing anyone sneaking aboard with a handy weapon?" Turns out these are belaying pins, stout wooden dowels that fit into holes, usually along the railing, that are used to tie (or "belay") ropes. Instead of tediously untying the knot, you just have to pull the pin and the line is free. One suspects, watching the movies, that if everybody pulled all the belaying pins for a fight, before they could start swinging, the sails would come plummeting down from the masts and cover everyone on deck.

Bilge – As noted above ("Bilge rat") the bilge is the lowest spot in the boat. The bilge is filled with stinking, slimy bilge water. When someone spouts off in annoying manner, you can brand his talk "bilge."

Black spot – In the beginning of "Treasure Island," when the pirates tell Flint that they're coming to kill him, they do it by giving him the Black Spot, a piece of paper with nothing on it but one black circle. In fact, some pirates really did that.

Booty – A pirate's ill-gotten gains. The word has taken on a new connotation – a shapely posterior – but that still works in the context of Talk Like a Pirate Day. In fact, we briefly marketed women's underwear with the slogan "Pirate Booty" across the back, but – sadly – they didn't sell terribly well.

Bowsprit – The forward pointing spar at the bow of the ship.

Brace – Two or more of a firearm or cannon. While we typically think of a brace of pistols, for example, as being two, one for either hand, the important part of the definition is "or more." Blackbeard, for example, carried six pistols. All the cannon on the left side of the ship might be referred to as "the port brace," even if it numbered 10 or 20 pieces.

Brass monkey – A brass base with 16 indentations for cannon balls, laid out in a square. This allowed a pyramid of 30 cannon balls to be stored near the guns without fear of their rolling about loose on the deck. Brass contracts faster and to

33

a greater degree than iron, which the ammunition was made of, so when the temperature dropped too far too quickly, the brass indentations would shrink so much that the iron cannon balls would come right off the monkey. This is the source of the phrase "It's cold enough to freeze the balls off a brass monkey."

Broadside – When two ships fought, they maneuvered so that they could fire all the guns from one side of the ship at their opponent at the same time, thus vastly increasing the chance that one might actually hit the other.

Bung hole – Victuals on a ship, particularly the water and rum, were stored in wooden casks. The stopper in the barrel is called the bung, and the hole is called the bung hole. That's all. It sounds a lot worse than it is, doesn't it? When sitting down for a meal on Talk Like a Pirate Day you might say, "Well, let's see what crawled out of the bung hole!" This remark will be followed by the sound of your companions putting down their cutlery and backing away from the table. Good! More for you!

Cannon – The ordnance on ships of the day tended to be somewhat diverse, not just on pirate ships but even in the Queen's Navy or the Spanish fleet. In the 15th and 16th centuries it was a rare artillery piece that could be counted on to throw two balls the same distance in more than the same general direction. The likelihood that two cannon on the same ship would be fairly evenly matched was almost nil. Add to that the slight vagaries between the size and shape of each ball (this was long before the concept of mass production) and you begin to see why a pirate's best chance was to get as close alongside a ship as possible and trade broadsides. Once the prey was disabled, they could board and capture her.

Cat 'o' nine tails – A particularly vicious whip used for flogging. The cat was also sometimes known as "the captain's daughter." In the old sea chantey, "What Do You Do With a Drunken Sailor," there is the line, "Give him a taste of the captain's daughter." Turns out what the song is calling for is a lot less pleasant than you thought, huh?

Chantey – A sea song, usually with a hearty chorus useful for setting a rhythm for tedious, menial scut work.

Chumbucket – Chum is fish bait, usually ground-up, oily fish, often with blood and guts. It's spread over the water to attract feeding fish, which are then caught. The fish seem to like it. In his book *Shark Trouble!* author Peter Benchley tells of an old Aussie skipper who chummed the waters with quartered horses to draw great whites. And the chumbucket, obviously, is the bucket the chum is kept in. Referring to something – say, a restaurant or bowl of chowder or your sister-in-law's meticulously clean bathroom – as a chumbucket is clearly not a compliment, although guys will find the concept irresistible.

Cutlass – Not something you drive, a cutlass is the weapon of choice among pirates. A cutlass is a short, heavy, curved sword with a single edge.

Crow's nest – A platform, sometimes enclosed, at the highest point of a ship, on which a lookout or two would perch. In your case, pretty much anytime you're going to go upstairs or to the restroom (it works either way), you might say you're going to visit the crow's nest.

Davey Jones Locker – The bottom of the sea, specifically the watery grave of drowning victims. Why Davey Jones? You will read occasionally someone claiming authoritatively that it refers to this person or that, but the truth is no one really knows. We can say with certainty that it has nothing to do with the onetime Monkees' heartthrob.

Deadlights – Eyes. Not sure where this one came from, but we like it a lot. "Damn yer deadlights," you might say as your friend beats you in yet another game of darts.

Deck – Technically this is the part of the ship you stand on. But you're not on a ship. There's a good probability the biggest ship you've ever been on was a canoe back at Boy Scout camp when you were a kid. For your purposes, the deck is the floor, because any sea dog worth his salt would never call any floor anything other than a deck. And, typically, the thing you do with the deck is "swab" it. (See below, "swab.")

Doubloon – A Spanish gold coin. Worth two pistoles. Don't ask us what a pistole was worth. We'll say "half a doubloon."

Dungbie – Rear end. Whether the ship's or a pirate's we have no idea. It's just a word we picked up somewhere and were told on relatively good authority that it's a pirate word. Sounds Scottish.

Fathom – A unit of measurement that, in the days of the Caribbean pirates, tended to be somewhat flexible. It's about six feet, with the emphasis on "about." To measure a line, sailors of the time would grab it, extending it from the tip of the outstretched right hand to the tip of the outstretched left. One fathom. Imagine the difference in fathoms if your crew included, say, Shaquille O'Neil and Willie Shoemaker.

Figurehead – Not a reference to your boss, although it's close. The figurehead is the carved figure at the front of the ship. Vikings (and they were fine pirates, aye!) used dragons. The English preferred figures of women. The Chinese often painted eyes on the bows of their ships to help them see in the dark.

Foc's'le – The dictionary calls it "a variant of forecastle." We call it one of our very favorite nautical words, if for no other reason than it's hard to say and hard to understand if you're not a mariner – it's "the section of the upper deck of a ship located at the bow forward of the foremast" if that helps you at all – yet as nautical sounding a word as there is.

Galley – The area of the ship where the cooking takes place. Refer to any kitchen as a galley and you'll be right in pirate style.

Gibbet – A wooden framework or cage from which dead pirates were hung as an example to others. On September 19th, anytime you're in a position of public display, you might say you're in a gibbet.

Glory hole – Our very favorite name for the privy.

Grog – Usually water with rum in it. We've had several people argue with us on this, saying grog is straight rum, or rum with a little water, or several other variations. But we're sticking by our guns on this one. When you consider that water on a ship was stored for long periods of time in slimy wooden barrels, you can see why a rum was added to each sailor's ration – to kill the rancid taste. In the context of Talk Like a Pirate Day you could use it to refer to any alcoholic beverage other than beer, and we aren't prepared to be picky about that, either. Call your beer grog if you want. We won't stop you!

Gunwales, or gunnels – The upper edge or wall of the side of the ship, so called because the guns were mounted on it. Try using it in reference to any high partition, including the side of the booth in a bar or restaurant, or your cubicle at work.

Hempen halter – The hangman's noose. When celebrating Talk Like a Pirate Day at work, you could use the phrase to refer to the tie you have knotted around your neck.

Hornpipe – Both a single-reeded instrument sailors often had aboard ship, and a spirited dance that sailors do. We don't have a lot to say on the subject, other than to observe that the common term for being filled with lust is "horny," and hornpipe then has some comical possibilities. "Is that a hornpipe in your pocket, or are you just glad to see me?"

Jack Ketch – The hangman. To dance with Jack Ketch means the same as to dance the hempen jig. Was there a real Jack Ketch, who was a particularly notorious or busy hangman who gave his name to the trade? We don't know, but it's possible. As a side note, John's mother's maiden name was Lynch, and he likes to imagine there was a hangman in the family tree somewhere.

Jolly Roger – The pirate flag, featuring the skull and crossbones over a black field. Many pirate ships had their own distinctive version of this basic flag, so you could tell at a glance if a particular pirate was bearing down on you. And here's another place where we know more than we're comfortable with, but feel a need to pass this knowledge on to you (hoping you might have some idea what to do with it.) The words Jolly Roger may (we say MAY, because no one knows for sure) come from the French words "joli rouge," meaning pretty red, a description of the bloody banner flown by early privateers. This term was corrupted to "Jolly Roger" by English buccaneers and was later applied to the black flag. Who knows? That could even be right.

Kelp – Seaweed.

Knot – A unit of speed, one nautical mile per hour. A nautical mile is longer than a statute (or land) mile. A nautical mile equals 1.15 miles on land. There must be a perfectly logical reason for the difference. We think it has to do with the fact that sailors drink a lot.

Kraaken – A legendary sea monster, usually described as a giant squid with tentacles and suckers and ... Eeeeuw!

League – A nautical unit of measurement equivalent to 3 nautical miles. Just to confuse things further.

Letter of marque – A document from the government that turned a pirate into a privateer, a ship with government sanction to raid the shipping of other countries. This didn't mean their activities were any more legal in the sense of international law, nor were captured privateers treated any more leniently than their unsanctioned brethren. The line between privateer and pirate was a thin one indeed, and many was the privateer (including some of the most notorious, such as Captain Kidd) who crossed it without realizing it until later.

Lubber hole – A hole through the platform surrounding the upper part of a ship's mast, through which one may climb to get aloft. We suppose this got the name because a true seaman didn't need the help, but could probably clamber over without the aid, or at least claim to, while a lubber, if he actually made it that high, needed a hole to squeeze through. For the purpose of Talk Like a Pirate Day, the lubber hole would be any tight entry, especially if it helped you get somewhere that might otherwise be difficult, like a shortcut to the men's room in a crowded bar.

Lubber line – A line or mark on the compass that shows the heading of the ship. You could use it in reference to any visual guide that helps you find your way, for instance, using the light post you parked next to as a help in finding your car.

Madagascar – A large island off the east coast of Africa, a favorite hangout of pirates working in the Indian Ocean raiding the shipping of the Grand Mogul of India and the British East India Company.

Mizzenmast – A secondary mast of the ship. You'd think from the name it might have been set in the middle (mizzen?) of the ship, but you'd be wrong. That's the mainmast. It strikes us that perhaps some speech therapy or at least orthodontia might have cleared up communications aboard ship, but our language would be less colorful for it.

Moses' Law – 40 lashes with the cat o' nine tails, minus one, which works out to 39 lashes. That's the same number of lashes Pilate ordered for Christ, so to give a man more than that would be un-Christian, although it's hard to imagine pirates caring too much about that. The fact is, 39 lashes are plenty, easily enough to kill. Typically fewer lashes were ordered or administered except for the most serious offenses. The trick seems to have been to make the recipient pass out with pain as quickly as possible to spare him a possible death.

On the account – Someone who is "on the account" has turned to the piratical life.

Piece of eight – A large, silver Spanish coin. It was worth eight "reals." Some were actually perforated into eight pie-shaped wedges, and could be broken into "bits," which could be spent individually. Two of these pieces made up one fourth, or one quarter, of the coin. This is why we sometimes refer to a quarter today as "two bits" (as in the old cheer, "Two bits, four bits, six bits, a dollar ...") For the record, we're pretty sure this one is true. We saw it in *National Geographic* magazine when we were kids.

Pirate rounds, The – The route from the Spanish Main to the Indian Ocean. On September 19th, it might well be the round of bars you stop at to celebrate.

Plank – That thing from which pirates were reputed to make captives walk, hands bound, into the drink. The fact that there is little or no evidence that they actually did this is immaterial. Thanks to literally hundreds of movies and books, it is firmly embedded in pirate lore and nothing can be done – either by a couple of louts like ourselves or by prissy, purse-lipped academics – to ever change that. There is some suggestion that the first pirates to actually make someone walk the plank got the idea from reading a book.

Plunder – Another word for booty or loot.

Poop - Here's the ultimate test of your Pirattitude. Have somewhere between three and seven beers, talking like a pirate the whole time. Then use the word "poop" and see if you can avoid giggling. For the record, the poop is the superstructure at the stern of the ship, typically where you'd see the captain standing, looking dramatic.

Prow – The nose or front of the ship. Its use when describing a well-endowed woman is obvious.

Quarter – Mercy – and rare was the pirate who took or gave quarter. In sitting around talking smack with your pirate buddies, give no quarter. Incidentally, there is a magazine called *No Quarter* written for pirate aficionados. Ironically, *No Quarter* magazine comes out quarterly. Go figure.

Quarterdeck – The stern portion of the upper deck of the ship.

Rum – The essential drink of pirates, and the basis of song and story. And, coincidentally, the liquor on which John first got drunk lo these many years ago. He hasn't been able to drink rum since, because of the visceral recollection of throwing it up later. But if Craig and Owen, twin brothers and John's high school classmates who served him that drink, are out there reading this, he still remembers you fondly for it.

Salmagundi – A dish of chopped meat, eggs, anchovies, onions and perhaps whatever else was lying around aboard ship. A pirate favorite. It's not likely to be on the menu at your favorite eatery, but you could easily appropriate the word for your own uses, say, to describe a giant pizza with everything.

Scut – A small crack or chink in the deck.

Scut work – Any tedious, usually maddeningly detailed work, like scraping the hull or polishing the brass. Today that could run the gamut from doing the inventory at a hardware store to almost any household task you could name - dishes, laundry, cleaning the grout, you get the idea.

Scuttlebutt – Rumor, innuendo. For the love of cheese, when you walk into a bar next September 19th, don't say "Wassup?" or anything like that. Say, "What's the scuttlebutt?"

Scurvy – This is a shipboard disease caused by improper nutrition. The word goes particularly well with dog. "Ye scurvy dog ye!" (Technically, it is caused by a diet deficient in vitamin C, and is characterized by spongy, bleeding gums, bleeding under the skin, and weakness. If that helps at all in your use of the term.)

Sea legs – Sailors, by definition, spend a lot of time at sea. They are conditioned to unconsciously adjust themselves to the rising and falling of the boat in heavy weather. This ability is described as "having good sea legs." What's particularly amusing is to watch people with good sea legs just after they disembark. Often they keep adjusting to the rising and falling, even when they're on dry land.

Seven Seas – Don't get caught in the trap of trying to name the Seven Seas. It's a sucker bet. "Uh, the Caribbean. The Mediterranean ... Uh, ..." There aren't seven in particular. The Seven Seas means all the oceans of the world. Trying to name them quickly identifies you as a lubber who has no business talking like a pirate.

Skull and crossbones – You know what this is. It's the universal symbol of pirates. Also known as the Jolly Roger, it is the flag that really flew over many a pirate ship, and showed that the ship bearing down on the harmless prey would give or take no quarter.

Spanish Main – The coastal region of Spanish America in the 16th and 17th centuries. It spread roughly from the Isthmus of Panama to the mouth of the Orinoco River in

Venezuela. (OK, we admit it. We looked that one up.)

Spar – A wooden or metal pole attached to the mast to support a sail. In other words, the sideways parts sticking out from the mast.

Spyglass – A telescope, usually one that can be comfortably held in the hands making it not much use for actually looking at far-away things while standing on a heaving quarterdeck.

Treasure – Call it booty, call it plunder, call it what you will, this is what being a pirate is all about.

West Indies – The islands separating the Caribbean Sea from the Atlantic Ocean. These include the Bahamas and the Antilles (greater and lesser, although all the Antilles seem pretty great to us).

Yardarm – The yard was a long spar slung to the mast of a ship to support and spread the mainsail. The yardarm is either end of the yard, which could be used to hang things or winch them onto the ship. There was a rule in polite company that it wasn't proper to drink before the sun was over the yardarm – in other words, until afternoon. We've always felt, and the pirates seemed to agree, that if the sun wasn't over the yardarm, the only proper thing to do was move to the other side of the yardarm, check out the sun again, and then open a bottle of beer.

Zanzibar – An island off the eastern coast of Africa. Use it in the sense of an exotic locale. "I'm off to Zanzibar," you might say when leaving for work. Or when leaving work.

Things you can do

Bass – Sounds like a fish. Actually, it was a fairly unpleasant things pirates really did to one another. When they caught one of their company stealing from them, the crew would leave the offender on Bass Island, a desolate, waterless sandbar. They would leave him with a day's supply of water and a pistol with one shot, and sail away. They'd let him think about it and decide how he wanted to go. As we said, it was fairly unpleasant, but these really were not nice people.

Belay – Shut up! Specifically, belay means to tie off. (See "belaying pin," above) "Belay that line!" the captain might shout so as to prevent the yardarm from falling. In a broader sense, it means stop what you're doing, and this is where it fits most neatly into pirate lingo. "Belay that talk," you'd yell at your friend as he's about to blurt out to your girlfriend what you said to the twin cocktail waitresses last night.

Blow me down – A favorite expression of Popeye's, this is an exclamation of surprise. A sailor with good sea legs could stand up in the strongest gale. If something COULD blow him down, that would be quite surprising. So this is a phrase to be used when you receive really surprising news ("Your ex-wife called and said she decided it was all her fault so she's giving back all the money." Your reply is, "Well blow me down!") But remember that it obviously has another connotation in this day and age, and that gives it great comic potential.

Careen – Careening was one of those things you had to do periodically to keep a ship floating, but to do it you had to get the ship out of water, and that made it pretty dangerous to pirates. The ship would be run aground in a shallow bay, then the pirates would wait for the tide to go down, exposing as much of the hull as possible. The ship would be pulled to one side, using block and tackle and brute strength, and the exposed surface would be scraped clean of barnacles and other debris, which hurt speed and maneuverability. The planks would then be pitched or tarred or painted. The ship would be pulled over to the other side and the process repeated. As you can imagine, it was long and difficult work, and the time spent with the ship on the beach was time the pirates were exposed without much chance to defend themselves. That's why they chose the most secluded, private places they could find to careen the ship. Put those two ideas together – repair and privacy – and the use of this word on Talk Like a Pirate Day is obvious: When you have to go to the restroom. "I've gotta go careen the hull," you might say as you lurch off for the glory hole.

Dance the hempen jig – Dangle from the end of a rope, be hanged.

Haul a jib – Pout. It obviously has a specific nautical meaning, a jib being a sail and haul being something you do with a sail. But "to haul a jib" has taken on the meaning of pouting or frowning, and we're damned if we know why.

Haul in the mainsheet – Sailor talk for some nautical thing that pirates and other sailors did involving sails. You're not likely to ever actually do this. But you could use it in other colorful ways, including commenting that a friend's shirt tail is out ("Dave, time to haul in the mainsheet."), his fly is open ("Whoa, Dave! Time to haul in the mainsheet!") or it's time to go ("Well, Dave. I guess it's time to haul in the mainsheet.") It also has potential for being used in a sexual way, but we'll leave that up to you.

Heave to – Drop (or heave, get it?) anchor and come to a halt.

Hornswoggle – Cheat. Frankly, we weren't aware of this being particularly piratical – sounds more like a word from the Wild West to us – but we found enough references to make its inclusion here plausible, and it certainly has a fine ring to it.

Keelhaul – Pirates punished people they didn't like by dragging them under the barnacle-encrusted keel. Besides being underwater for a period of time far too long to be comfortable, the recipients were also usually cut up by the sharp-edged barnacles growing on the hull. We've heard two different descriptions of how this was done, either tossing the bound victim off the bow and letting the ship sail over him from bow to stern, or tossing him off one side and hauling him by rope under the hull and back up the other side. We are not in a position to judge which was the actual process, but we don't think we'd care for either one to be done to us or anyone we call shipmate.

Measure for chains – To be outfitted for the gibbet cage (see "Gibbet" above.) Since the gibbet cage was largely used to hold dead people or people who were soon to be dead, this was not a good thing to be measured for. You might use it in the sense of being set up: "Looks like I'm being measured for chains," you might say as you notice your co-workers setting you up to take the blame for something.

Plunder – Loot, raid or otherwise attack a prize and make off with the goods on board. It can also be a noun describing what was taken. So you can plunder the plunder, but that sounds a little redundant, so we prefer plunder the loot or loot the plunder.

Shiver me timbers – When the wind blows, when the gale is at full force, or when the enemy's broadsides are striking with alarming accuracy, the pirates' ship shudders so strongly that the very timbers may be said to shiver. Thus the phrase. It's used in the same sense as "blow me down," an expression of surprise, even incredulity or alarm. Interestingly, timbers appear to be the only thing that can be shivered. We've never heard, for instance, a person say "Shiver me yardarm" or "Shiver me chum." It just doesn't work. Timbers could almost be defined as, "The things that are shivered."

46

Smartly – Do something quickly. "Smartly, me lass," you might say when sending the waitress off for another round. She will be so impressed she might well spit in your beer.

Splice the mainbrace – We are given on good authority that this means "have a drink," as in "Let's drop anchor in that alehouse and splice the mainbrace." We have to confess we have no idea why it might mean this, or what splicing the mainbrace might really mean. It sounds like some repair work you might have to do to some really important thing, and if you're really in need of a drink, that could be a reasonable metaphor. Yeah, that could be it.

Stow – Put away. You can use it in the sense of 'stop that" or "shut up." "Stow that talk, ya bilge rat."

Swab – Mop, as in "Swab the deck!" Certainly other things could be swabbed, but in our minutes of intensive research we don't recall ever hearing of anyone swabbing anything else. Still, good pirate verbs are hard to come by, and in the next section we'll show you how this can be used to some comic effect. A swab or swabby is also a less-than-complimentary way to refer to a sailor, the indication being that all he is good for is mopping up after the "real" pirates have done the hard work.

Swing the lead – Sailors measured the distance to the bottom by throwing out a measured line with a lead weight. Knowing how far it is to the sea floor or a coral reef is important if you don't want the bottom ripped out of your ship. That could be embarrassing to any pirate. Now they have sonar and other electronic gizmos, but swinging the lead is a more time-honored phrase. Use it when you're trying to determine a distance.

Tales, dead men tell no – Blackbeard was the pirate credited with the practice of taking his treasure ashore with a single sailor, burying it, then killing his assistant and throwing him in the hole before covering it up. That way he would be the only one who knew precisely where the treasure was hidden. We presume after the first few times Blackbeard and a sailor rowed ashore to bury treasure and ol' Teach came back alone, the rest of the crew figured out this was not a good shore duty to be volunteering for.

Take a caulk – Rest. The spaces between planks of a deck were caulked, or filled with a putty or tar, to keep them watertight. Just like today's tourist aboard a Carnival cruise ship, pirates liked to stretch out in the sun when they had some free time and nap on the deck. Unlike Carnival cruisers, they would often get lines of caulk on their back.

Walk the plank – One way to get off a ship, obviously not the best way. Making a bound prisoner walk off the end of a plank over the railing and fall into the ocean. Invariably fatal. As we noted earlier, there is little or no evidence that pirates actually did this, but that hasn't stopped it from becoming enshrined in lore.

Weigh anchor – Raise the anchor and store it so you can be on your way. As you rise from the table where you've been celebrating Talk Like a Pirate Day say, "Well, mateys, time for me to weigh anchor." And time for us to weigh anchor on this section of the book.

Chapter 6

Now, the fun begins

Now you know the basics, and, if you're feeling creative, the real fun can begin. Putting this many phrases together in new, creative ways is the – dare we say it? – artistic part of Talk Like a Pirate Day, and the most fun.

It couldn't be easier. Take any of the things that can be done, say, "Dance the hempen jig," and match it up with a thing that a person can be, or even a thing that is a thing. You can either dip randomly into the previous chapter, coming up with verbs and adjectives as fate throws them to you, or, if you're feeling a little nervous about getting started, just use the handy chart we have thoughtfully provided.

Mix and match

Column a	(ye) column b	column c
1 Walk the plank	scurvy	sea dog
2 Swab the deck	kelp-eating	kraaken
3 Haul in the mainsheet	barnacle-encrusted	bilge rat
4 Belay that	rum-soaked	corsair
5 Weigh anchor	chum-swilling	freebooter
6 Stow that bilge	swashbuckling	wench
7 Blow me down	keelhauling	skipper
8 Hornswoggle me	careening	lubber
9 Take a caulk	hornpipe-dancing	buccaneer
10 Dance the hempen jig	chantey singing	bos'n

Just pick one at random from each column. The middle column of modifiers was adapted from the "things that you can be" list. It's legitimate, really.

You could even make a game of it. Have friends take turns calling out numbers and watch the fun begin!

Now that our handy grid has gotten you started, it's time to try your hand "freestyle," as it were, in your everyday life. Are you up to it? Of course you are, me bucko! Haul anchor and set sail for the adventure that is Talk Like a Pirate Day!

Around the house

For those of you with wives or girlfriends (or both), some care must be taken as to which pirate terms you employ with your "significant other." Some women are less open to the jocularity of guy humor than others. You probably already have a good feeling for whether you can call your mate a wench or not. If you try it and she takes offense, quickly remind her that wench simply means a girl or woman, as we noted above, without necessarily having any negative connotation. If she smiles slyly and inquires about your yardarm or hornpipe, well, you don't need our help.

If wench is out, definitely stick to "me beauty." Hard as this may be to believe, some women actually find the concept of talking like a pirate for extended periods stupid. But even most in this category can't resist it when you call them "me beauty." And if they do, do you really want to pursue the relationship?

Some of you, maybe the vast majority, will have significant others who actually enjoy Talk Like a Pirate Day, who get into the spirited back-and-forth of the event.

All the same, the most tolerant and even playful spouse will draw the line somewhere. John's wife, Tori, for example, loves football and fishing and beer and is quite the good sport, all while maintaining a devastating sexuality and fiery temper that combine to make her the perfect woman. But not even John is so stupid as to walk into the house and tell her, "Wench, get in the galley and swab the deck or I'll fire a broadside right up your porthole." If he did, he'd be picking pieces of eight out of his yardarm for a week.

Watch it, is all we're saying. Know your significant other, and address her accordingly. And, you know, this is probably good advice every day of the year, not just on Talk Like a Pirate Day.

WARNING: It goes without saying (but we'll say it anyway, it's that important) most women do not consider the phrase "Prepare to be boarded!" an adequate substitute for foreplay. Really, you'd be amazed at how ineffective this is.

A final note - In the house, the kitchen is the galley, the bathroom is the glory hole, and pretty much anyplace else can be referred to as "the poop," but only if you can keep from giggling.

At the office

Except for your favorite local tavern, there's no better place to practice talking like a pirate than at work.

Because, of course, it's totally inappropriate, at least in any setting where you're likely to interact with the public. In a private office, in a factory setting, perhaps even at a gas station, it will be OK. At the offices of National Public Radio one September 19th, for instance, employees logging into the service's private intranet were greeted by a picture of the president of NPR wearing an eye patch and carrying a parrot on his shoulder.

But typically, in a work situation where you interact with other people, there's an expectation you'll behave in an appropriately buttoned-down way. So imagine the attention you'll attract when the phone rings and, instead of saying, "Johnson and Eckers, attorneys," you bellow, "Avast there, matey! We be lawyers! Who can we scuttle for ya today?" or leap up from the conference table and tell the guy who just disagreed with you, "Ya scurvy dog! Belay that talk, or you'll be dancing the hempen jig!"

Try it. It's easy. It's fun. And how much do you really like that job, anyway?

A couple of cautions. First, pirate talk does have a certain sauciness, as you will have noticed by now, and in the wrong environment – that is to say, almost anything outside a locker room – one person's wacky, fun-loving manliness is another's sexual harassment, which, as we all know, is actionable. So let's keep things in control, guys. Neither Mark nor John particularly wants to be hauled into court as an accessory. Second, a big part of the fun of talking like a pirate is tossing around denigrating put-downs in a friendly, obscure way, so that the recipient, usually some bud, has to think about it for a second to figure out he's been insulted. This might not be the best tactic with your boss, especially if he or she is anything like some of the bosses we've had. There are ways, of course, to get in your digs ("skipper" is one safe dodge) and, if that fails and the boss actually catches on that "kelp-festooned kraaken" isn't exactly a compliment, you'll have to feign ignorance. "It means what? That? Oh, gosh, I thought it was an affectionate reference to a wise old seaman." That'll leave a bad taste in your mouth.

With that out of the way, let's see how a typical business conversation might go if translated into pirate talk. On any other day, let's say February 23rd, the conversation might go like this:

> *Boss: Hello, Doug.*
> *Doug: Yes, boss?*
> *Boss: Do you have the new figures on the Driscoll account ready?*
> *Doug: I'll have that for you by this afternoon.*
> *Boss: There's been a change. You need to factor in our real costs, not the figures we've been using.*
> *Doug: OK, sir. Any extension on the deadline?*
> *Boss: No. Now, don't let me down. The whole firm is counting on you. If you need me, call my secretary. I'll be out on the golf course.*
> *Doug: Yes, sir, you can depend on me.*

On September 19th, that same conversation might sound something like this.

> *Boss: Ahoy there, you scurvy sea dog.*
> *Doug: Aye, skipper?*
> *Boss: Have you finished that scut work I gave you?*

Doug: You'll be readin' it by the time the sun's over the yardarm.
Boss: Not anymore. The wind's shifted, and we have to scuttle our
plans to hornswoggle the lubbers.
Doug: Arrr! We still attack at dawn?
Boss: Aye. Now get to work or we'll keelhaul ya. I'm off to
Zanzibar.
Doug: Aye aye, ya great grog-soaked lubber.

Trolling in taverns

The whole point of Talk Like a Pirate Day is to have fun, and what could be more fun than testing your pirate panache for picking up members of the opposite sex at parties, taverns and other such locales? (Although if you want to use them to pick up members of the same sex, we won't stop you. After all, see "Brethren of the Coast" in the chapter on lingo.)

With that in mind, we offer this list of the Top Pickup Lines for use on International Talk Like a Pirate Day. Some of these work better from men to women. A few work best woman to man. But most of them, we truly believe, are gender-neutral. For instance, we can't think of a better pickup line on September 19th (or really, any night) than "Prepare to be boarded!" And while it's never worked particularly well (actually, none of these has worked particularly well, but we'll keep on trying) we know that it would certainly be effective if a woman came up and said it to us.

There are plenty more. Here's just a sample.

Avast, me proud beauty! Wanna know why my Roger is so Jolly?
Have ya ever met a man with a real yardarm?
Come on up and see me urchins.
Yes, that is a hornpipe in my pocket and I am happy to see you.

I'd love to drop anchor in your lagoon.

Pardon me, but would ya mind if I fired me cannon through your porthole?

How'd you like to scrape the barnacles off me rudder?

Ya know, darlin', I'm 97 percent chum-free.

Well blow me down?

They don't call me Long John because my head is so big.

You're drinking a Salty Dog? How'd you like to try the real thing?

Wanna shiver me timbers?

Mind if I swing from your rigging?

I've sailed the Seven Seas, and you're the sleekest schooner I've ever sighted.

Brwaack! Polly want a cracker? ... Oh, wait. That's for Talk Like a PARROT Day.

That's the finest pirate booty I've ever laid eyes on.

Let's get together and haul some keel.

That's some treasure chest you've got there.

Well, as you can see, there's really no limit to pirate pickup lines. Just get out there and lay some nautical talk upon your intended and watch the sparks fly. But remember, if there's a positive response (it could happen!), you've got to be prepared to back up yer talk with action. So don't promise more than you can deliver.

At Sporting Events

What are the odds? The first year that Talk Like a Pirate Day achieves international attention, the NFL's Super Bowl pits two pirate teams against one another. The Tampa Bay Buccaneers scuttled the favored Oakland Raiders in Super Bowl XXXVII by the score of XLVIII-XXI.

On the Friday evening before the big game, one intrepid reporter, Evan Grant from the *Dallas Morning News*, looking for a way to write something different about the upcoming contest, thought of the "pirate" angle and remembered some fuss about the pirate day last fall. He had actually saved the Dave Barry article and used it to track us down. This is an important tip for you boys and girls who are considering becoming big time journalists yourself. A bigger tip for those boys and girls would be: Find a new career goal. But we digress.

Grant gave us a call, seeking some appropriate piratical phrases that fans could yell out at appropriate moments during the game. Here's what showed up in his column that Sunday morning, no doubt to the bemusement if not downright bewilderment of the Dallas reading public.

"Arrrrr, he scuttled the secondary." Long run or pass

"There's nothin' left but to breach the fore and mizzen-mast." Fourth down, time to kick a field goal.

"Arr, you could use him to plug a cannon hole during a broadside!" To be used in reference to a rather large player.

"Slap weasel grease to it and fight on." Reference to an injured player who needs to return to the game. Now, we admit that there's no record anywhere of pirates actually using weasel grease, or even the word weasel. Nor are we aware of anyone actually using weasels as a source of grease. But it sounds funny. Say it a couple of times. "Weasel grease. Weasel grease." That's good enough for us.

"One more like that and ye'll dance a hempen jig." Player penalized for unsportsmanlike celebration.

"Arr, the lubber be diggin' fer buried treasure." Player adjusts his cup.

"They stranded him thar on the Isle of Bass with nought but his britches and his mother's eyes." Pass pocket broke down and left

the quarterback defenseless.

"A Hook (and lateral), A Hook (and lateral) My Kingdom for a Hook! (and lateral)" Technically, that's a Shakespearean reference, but the Hook thing is pure pirate. And since there are no NFL teams called the Bards or the Fighting Thespians, we'll have to take what we can get. It means, "My team desperately needs a trick play."

And, finally, *"Now, thar be a chumbucket baptism!"* The players have doused the coach with the Gatorade bucket. And sure enough, as the clock ticked away, Buccaneer head coach Jon Gruden was awash in the stuff – a true "chumbucket baptism."

Is that all? Arrr! We know what ye be thinkin'! "Sure, that's just peachy for football, but don't you have any phrases for any of the other sports?" Stand fast thar, ya lubber! Try these phrases on during your other sporting events!

Baseball: Of all sports we know, baseball may be the most pirate friendly. In Pittsburgh, there's even a team called the Pirates (who have sucked for several decades, although we Pirate Guys are certainly pulling for them this season.) There's also their milder counterparts in Seattle, the Mariners. There are already some well-established piratish terms in baseball like "the ball sailed on him" or "around the horn." But let us suggest some other phrases that might be helpful for the pirate-talking baseball enthusiast.

"Thar be a Spaulding Tattoo on that white orb!" To be used in reference to a well-hit ball.

"The cannons be ready as this ship prepares another pass." We have reached the "heavy hitter" section of the batting order.

"That be ALL WIND and NO SAIL!" Player takes a big cut but misses the ball.

"Arrr, he be caught drifting toward St. Kitts when he should have

been staying in at harbor!" Baserunner picked off by pitcher.

"Blast ye! A cannon shot right in the poop deck!" Batter gets hit by a pitch ... especially in the fleshy part of the hip.

"Great Neptune! Thar she blows! Out, out beyond the horizon!" Home run!

Hockey: Hockey is a great sport. The players move like individual ships on a smooth sea with a brisk wind ... occasionally slamming into one another and leaving a pool of blood on the icy surface. Very pirate-like, indeed! We can't explain "icing" to you or pronounce all those French Canadian names, nor do we have a clue what the blue line is all about. But we can suggest some pirate phrases you might try.

"Thar young Jimmy sits in the brig while the skirmish rages on!" The player is in the penalty box while play continues.

"Arrr, thar be splinters for all in that!" Player has committed a high sticking offense.

"We've not seen the lads brawl like that since Toothless Mary closed her pub early!" A fight breaks out on the ice.

Basketball: There are NO PIRATE PHRASES for basketball. Alright, well, maybe there are, but we can't think of any. Pirate phrases usually depict the open spaces of a pirate's world, and basketball, bowling, curling and checkers don't easily make one think of the open sea and the smell of chum. OK, maybe bowling makes one think of chum, but only in a very abstract and offensive way.

We also acknowledge that there are hundreds of sports for which we have not developed pirate phrases. Soccer/football for example is perfect for pirate phrases as would be Rugby, Australian Rules Football, hurling, lacrosse ... the list goes on, but we do not. The key is not to read from a script, but to explore the potential of talking like a pirate and be ready to extemporize at a moment's notice! In short, do as we do; make it up as you go along.

At school

Chances are that September 19th is going to land on a school day more often than not. That's a lucky break for all the little buckos and their hearty teachers. And for all of you school administrators out there, it's a chance to try to administer the fun out of one more thing that may bring some joy to life. EVERYBODY WINS!

In the years since our little idea got sprung on the world, the reaction from educators has been overwhelming, so much so that we actually put a curriculum on our Web site. On September 19th, kids are sporting eye patches and plastic hooks while principals and superintendents are expelling them under the districts' "zero thought" policy.

Some teachers talk about parts of the world where pirates traveled and build geography lessons around that. Other educators examine pirate law and the conflict with international commerce. There is a whole world of "teachable moments" in Talk Like a Pirate Day. The possibilities are as boundless as the open sea.

Now, a word to our administrative friends, whom we kid because we love. Lighten up, for God's sake! One of our friendly principals delivered her morning announcements in a pirate voice and was a smash hit with staff and kids for weeks after. There must have been at least one principal who donned a tri-corner hat and declared him or herself the captain of the ship. Or perhaps a superintendent was referred to at a staff meeting as "Admiral Wobblebottom." Never miss a chance at whimsy.

The real lesson being taught is that part of being human is to have some fun built into our lives. So here's a few hints for making Talk Like a Pirate Day work in your school.

Students: Even if you haven't got a great grasp on the whole pirate lingo thing, you should really work to interject some "Arrs" (growling while you do it) as you say words with the letter "R" in them. For instance, instead of saying, "Good morning, Mr. Larson." Try saying, "Fine marrrrrnin' Mistarrrrr Larrrrrson!"

Remember, "aye" means "yes" and "aye aye" means "yes, I will do that right away," at least as far as we're concerned. Now, try saying, "Aye aye, Mistarrrrr Larrrrrrson!"

Kids, look. We know that the zero-thought policies are there for your protection and that a plastic hook or cutlass isn't going to hurt anyone, but you don't need to break the rules to enjoy the spirit of Talk Like a Pirate Day. You can make a hook with your finger and squint a whole bunch. Have fun, but respect the chain of command. There's a good pirate.

Teachers and Staff: You have fun, too. Remember, Talk Like a Pirate Day was invented by adults FOR adults. We are just including the kids because we can't seem to get rid of them, especially at school.

Save the sauciness for the staff room. Pirate humor is packed to the gunnels with double entendre not suitable for some children (who, of course, think we don't get it when THEY do it).

Be creative. Use piratespeak to illustrate proper usage of pronouns and verbs. Do treasure hunts and mapping exercises (maybe even incorporating compass directions, if you can remember how to do that) and reading. Do you know how many kids have NEVER READ "Treasure Island"?

Administration and support staff: Set a positive tone. We know, you ALWAYS do that, but today can be a day when kids and teachers alike see your playful side. What would it hurt if they caught you being silly?

Answer the phone with a hearty "Ahoy!" Sure, someone may be momentarily confused, but most people play along when you explain to them that it is Talk Like a Pirate Day.

Organize a Talk Like a Pirate contest. There may be some kids who struggle in other areas who may excel at something for the first time in their lives. This gives you a chance to recognize them.

Encourage creativity and playfulness. Embrace the chaos. Order will be restored by and by.

At church

Every few years, September 19th will be a day of worship. That's fine. You know, many of Jesus' followers were fishermen, the law-abiding cousin of the pirate. Talking like a pirate on "the Lord's day" is not sacrilegious but rather a reminder that God's love encompasses us all. Rich, poor, saint and sinner, we all need a good ol' fashioned revival from time to time.

Mark grew up Protestant – Baptist, as a matter of fact – so he knows a thing or two about church and hymn singin' and the like. He can still name the books of the Bible, mostly in order, and learned how to read King James' English before Dr. Seuss'. He sat in the pew with his little brother, Pauly, and flipped through the hymnal tacking the phrase, "in the bath tub," to the titles of the Great Hymns of the Faith. "We Have and Anchor," always cracked them up. There wasn't a Sunday School room at Galilee Baptist Church in which they hadn't been spanked.

Here are some suggestions for the whole church.

Pastor and deacons: Change up that opening/closing prayer a little. Instead of, "Dear Heavenly Father, we do thank Thee and praise Thee," try, "Ahoy, Almighty God, Admiral of the Universe!" Most folks know that "Amen" simply means, "so be it" so why not close out a prayer on September 19th with, "Aye aye, Cap'n!"?

When the collection plate is passed, instead of asking the congregation to, "Share of your bounty," ask them to "Share of ye booty."

Protestants, especially Baptists, already do a good job with, "thee, thou, thine and ye," all they have to do is add a little growl to their voice and they are right in the spirit of the day!

This would be a great day for a sermon on Jonah. Wasn't he thrown overboard by pirates? Could they be pirates just this week? C'mon. What would it hurt?

Music Minister and Choir: Your potential contributions to this day are tremendous! Think of the hymn selection: "We Have and Anchor" (as the Summers boys get carried off to an empty Sunday School classroom, giggling and screaming all the way,) "There is a Fountain," and do not let the day go by without singing, "How Great Thou Arrrrrrrrrrt!"

How about a nautical medley from the choir? For added effect, they could wear eye patches!

Introduce the pastor to the pulpit with a tin whistle? You will find out how many in the congregation were in the Navy by counting the heads of those people who stood at "attention" before the sermon.

Nursery staff (The unsung heroes of the church): Some construction paper and empty paper towel tubes and you have converted a crib or a playpen into a pirate ship! And isn't conversion what church is all about?

You could play, "Keelhaul the Lubber" by wrapping a bungee cord around a hyper toddler's waist and hanging him from a coat rack. But not if that's the week you're going to be inspected by the state child welfare officials.

"But what about the babies?" you ask, "They can't 'Talk' like a Pirate if they are preverbal." Too true. However, there is nothing cuter in the world than a baby with an eye patch. Except, perhaps, a whole nursery full of babies with eye patches.

In the doctor's office

Pirates need medical attention from time to time. Shark bites, cannonballs, belaying pins and cutlasses can all cause serious injury. As we get older, we have more skill at scheduling medical emergencies, or at least making an appointment. How about seeing the ship's surgeon on September 19th?

A doctor's office is nothing like the deck of a frigate, strewn with limbs and guts and puddles of chum. Rather, it is a sterile building with uncomfortable seating and a *People* magazine from November 1994. You will have to work very hard to bring the joy of Talk Like a Pirate Day to such a place as this, but we have faith in you.

Here are some tips for Talking Like a Pirate at the doctor's:

Refer to the nurses as, "me beauty" or "me angel of mercy." This applies to male nurses, too. Trust us on this.

When they weigh you (and they ALWAYS weigh you – you could come in with an arrow sticking out of your forehead and the first thing they'll do is weigh you) confess to overly generous portions of grog and hardtack. This will distract them as you take one foot off the scale and shift some of your girth to the floor. Gravity is no friend to "manly" pirates.

Consider the following exchange:

Nurse: All right, Mr. Blackbeard, please strip to the waist and the doctor will be right in.

Pirate Dude: You want me to hoist me mainsail, me beauty?

Nurse: Uh, yeah. Just take off your shirt.

Pirate Dude: Shall I lower me breeches so's the surgeon can have a peek at me poop deck?

Nurse: Oh! Uh, no, that won't be necessary for this visit. You did say you had a sore throat, didn't you, Mr. Blackbeard?

Pirate Dude: Aye, me hornpipe be swoggled, by Gar! And, as much as I've been feastin' on crabs, I think the crabs be feastin' on me! Arrr!

Nurse: Ewwww! Let me get you a paper gown and some insecticide.

Pirate Dude: Thar's a good wench. What'd ya be doin' later this fine evening?

Nurse: Let me reiterate, Mr. Blackbeard, ewwww!

Refer to the coldness of the stethoscope with a witty remark like, "Arrr, I love the feel of cold steel on me skin."

When asked to say, "ahhh," say, "Arr."

A proctological exam can be awkward for both the doctor and patient. Try lightening the mood with a comment like, "I'm being scuttled! Arrr!" or "Doc, you didn't say 'Prepare to be boarded,' did you?"

At some point, the doctor will tell you to "Turn your head and cough." When this happens, turn your head and spit. Extra points if you bring your own spittoon.

All of these behaviors will lighten the day for the doctor, nurses and that lady in the waiting room who glares at everyone who goes ahead of her.

Chapter 7

Music has charms

One of the very cool things about having created this holiday is the people we have met, at least electronically. Not just famous people like Dave Barry and the near-famous like the book agent for John Lithgow, or even the annoying publicist from a seafood restaurant chain that tried to hijack us (but that's a different story which we'd be happy to tell if you catch us while drinking, which is easy, but never mind). The holiday was announced from the stage during a Jimmy Buffett concert – by Jimmy Buffett! We haven't communicated with him, but we think that's pretty cool.

Hundreds of people have written to us to share their stories, to offer us pictures of themselves and their friends enjoying the holiday. Many write to tell us we're geniuses and stuff, and while we doubt that very much, it's certainly nice to hear.

Some have become, if not quite friends, at least regular correspondents whom we have come to know pretty well.

Comrades, even shipmates, ya might say.

One such kindred spirit is Tom Smith. Tom is a musician, a songwriter of a style called "filk music," which we won't try to explain because we don't understand it ourselves. If you look up his Web site (www.TomSmithOnline.com) you can learn more about it than we could ever tell you.

In any case, it turns out Tom is an incredibly gifted songwriter, and a darn fast one. He heard about Talk Like a Pirate Day on the day itself, September 19th, 2003. The next morning, while Ol' Chumbucket and Cap'n Slappy were nursing serious, near-fatal hangovers, we opened our e-mail to find a missive from Tom. After congratulating us for having had the idea and then taking it way too far, he said he had written this song the previous night and thought it was "about right." He didn't have the music yet, but said "you can hum it to almost any 3/4 pirate song, especially Steve Goodman's 'Lincoln Park Pirates.' "

All of that music stuff went completely over our heads. But the lyrics are perfect. They captured the whole spirit of the day as well as it can be captured. So with no further ado, but with Tom's permission and the note that he'll be putting it on a CD soon so you'll definitely want to go to his Web site and buy it, we present his ditty.

"TALK LIKE A PIRATE" DAY

Words and Music Copyright 2003 by Tom Smith
Dedicated ta Cap'n Slappy an' Ol' Chumbucket fer creatin' National
Talk Like A Pirate Day, September 19th

Most days are like all of the others,
Go to work, come back home, watch TV,
But, brother, if I had me druthers,
I'd chuck it and head out to sea,

For I dream of the skull and the crossbones,
I dream of the great day to come,
When I dump the mundane for the Old Spanish Main
And trade my computer for rum! ARRR!

T' me,
Yo, Ho, Yo, Ho,
It's "Talk Like A Pirate" Day!
When laptops are benches God gave us for wenches,
And a sail ain't a low price to pay!
When timbers are shivered and lillies are livered
And every last buckle is swashed,
We'll abandon our cars for a shipfull of ARRRs
And pound back the grog till we're sloshed.

(spoken) Anyone see my keys?
Just off the coast o' Florida, matey! ARRR!

Don't pick up yer phone and say "Hello,
Our ten-o-clock meeting's delayed,"
Ye scrunch up yer face and ye bellow,
"AVAST! Ye've been bleedin' BELAYED!"

Ye can't keep this fun to yourself, I bet,
So sing "Aye", "ARRR", and "Ayy", every man!
We ain't got much grasp of the alphabet,
But a damn good retirement plan! (raucous laughter)

T' me,
Yo, Ho, Yo, Ho,
It's "Talk Like A Pirate" Day!
Whatever's in fashion is in for a thrashin'
And bein' polite is passe!
When it's ev'ry man's duty to grab his proud beauty
And let out a hearty YO HO!
And if this offends you, hold your breath as we sends you
Ta Davy Jones' Locker ya go!

Where IS Davy Jones' Locker, anyway?
Right near Monkee Island! Arr, aye, arr....

We'll tell every banker "Heave to and weigh anchor!"
Buy latte with pieces of eight
We'll fight to be chosen as cap'n or bosun
The loser, o' course, is first mate!

When we hoist Jolly Roger the landlubbers dodge 'er,
We fill 'em with loathing and fear,
We'll plunder and pillage each city and village,
Or at least clean out Wal-Mart of beer!

Ahoy, mateys! And Welcome ta "Iron Chef Pirate!"
Let's see the secret ingredient!
(GONNNG) It's Barnacles!
Oh ho! That'll be some cutting-edge cuisine!

"AWK! AWK!" (bzzzzzz)
Hold still, Polly! I need this for me salad!
Avast there, me bucko! Ye need CARROT shavings! CARROT!
Oh, CARROT!
Aye! Heh heh heh... moron.

And you! WHAT are ye doin' with that salmon?
I'm grillin' it on a hunk o' cedar, what d'y'think?
Ye CAN'T do that in a JAPANESE STIR-FRY, ye bilge rat!
Oh HO! Ye never heard o' "wokkin' the plank"?

There ain't no computin' or morning commutin',
No "Parking Lot Full" signs for me,
No lawns ta be mowin' or bills to be owin',
I'm knowin' the pull of the sea.
The fresh salty brace of the wind on my face
Through hurricane, sunshine or squalls,
I'm keepin' my eyes on the distant horizon,
Verizon can hold all my calls!

To wear a red coat full o' buckles,
To earn a few duelling scars,
Well, at least we can get a few chuckles
By filling the office with ARRRs!
And maybe we'll never get closer,
Than watchin' 'em on the big screen,
So here's to old Errol and Depp as Jack Sparrow,
And every damn one in between!

T' me,
Yo, Ho, Yo, Ho,
It's "Talk Like A Pirate" Day!

That time in September when sea dogs remember
That grown-ups still know how ta play!
When wenches are curvy and dogs are all scurvy
And a software patch covers your eye,
Ta hell with our jobs, for one day we're all swabs
And buccaneers all till we die!

So hoist up the mainsils and shut down your brain cells,
They only would get in the way,
Avast there, me hearty, we're havin' a party,
It's "Talk Like A Pirate" Day!

All right, me buckos! We've got a NEW retirement plan!
What's it called, Cap'n?
A 401-ARRR!

Nice office, matey! Who designed it?
An ARRR-chitect!

I've got to stop at the store on the way home.
Where ye goin'? TARRRget?
No, MARRRshall Fields.

Incoming message, Cap'n!
(.-) Alpha... (.-.) Romeo... (.-.) Romeo... (.-.) Romeo...
Whose side are they on?
ARRR side, o' course!

(fade)

Now ye're pushin' it.
Oh, so I've gone too fARRR?

Created a monster, I have.
No, no, no. That's talkin' like Yoda....

(fade out)

Chapter 8

Piracy is as old as the sea, and many, many people, both male and female, have heeded the call of the sea and tried to make a living by preying on others. Bad, bad pirates!

Of the thousands who have done so, a few have been so successful or so appallingly evil that they have transcended their rude calling and become figures of myth. But they were real people. Here, in no particular order, are a few of our favorites, if favorite is the right word for people who achieved fame by their ability to kill and steal.

Blackbeard (Edward Teach) – The most notorious, infamous pirate of them all. A giant of his time, well over six feet tall, with an imposing beard, a maniacal light in his eyes and fearsome, imposing strength, Blackbeard was known for his cruelty, not just to his victims but to his own crew. He was capable of odd outbreaks of violence, once firing his pistol randomly under the table while dining with crew members, wounding one severely in the knee. When bored, he was known to call his crew to the bilge, where they would seal the doors and light stinkpots of sulfur to see which man could stand the stench of hell the longest. Naturally, it was always Blackbeard who was last to lurch out of the hellhole.

And if he behaved that way to his own crew, how do you imagine he treated his captives? Badly, to say the least.

Having made a fortune as a pirate, he tried to retire ashore, but he found life boring and returned to his thieving ways at sea. Finally hunted down, his ship was cornered by two British sloops under the command of Lieutenant Robert Maynard, on November 22nd, 1718. While some histories say Maynard killed Blackbeard in single combat, others – which seem more believable given the pirate's fearsome reputation – say that several of Maynard's crew joined in the melee. Blackbeard was shot at point-blank range but kept fighting. His face and hands were slashed, but the fight continued. A Highlander from Maynard's crew joined the fight and set about Blackbeard with his broadsword. The first blow cut Blackbeard's neck, and he cried out "Well done lad" the second mighty blow took off the pirate's head, which was hung from a pole for all to see as Maynard sailed back into port.

Captain Kidd – Another of the most notorious pirates, William Kidd had a pirating career that actually lasted only four years, beginning in April 1696, and the truth is, he may have gotten a bum rap. He set sail with letters of marque from King George, authorizing him to prey on Spanish and French shipping but making it clear he was to leave alone the ships of England and her allies. Somewhere along the way his crew got tired of the slim pickings. A mutiny was put down when Kidd killed the leader, William Moore, by hitting him with a bucket. The pressure mounted and Kidd's ship, whether by his command or under pressure from the crew, took prizes they were not entitled to as privateers.

Kidd was eventually deserted by his crew and tried to return to England with records that would supposedly clear him. Kidd made it to England, but the records got misplaced, and after a one-sided trial the captain was found guilty of murder (the death of Moore) and piracy. He was hanged in 1701.

In 1910, an American researching public records in London discovered the documents that had disappeared all those years before, which might have saved Captain Kidd's life.

Jean Lafitte – The last great pirate operating in American waters, Lafitte came to New Orleans from France in 1809 with his brother Pierre and immediately became involved in piracy and smuggling. Within a year Jean had become the leader of the pirate colony in Barataria Bay, an island stronghold near New Orleans, from which Lafitte's ships ruled the Gulf of Mexico.

During the War of 1812, Lafitte sided with the Americans. He was able to trade his assistance for a pardon and during the Battle of New Orleans he and his men fought alongside General Andrew Jackson. British forces were mowed down like field mice under the barrage of the pirates' guns. British casualties numbered more than 2,000 killed, while the Americans lost eight lives. The fact that the war had actually ended before the battle took place sort of spoils the story, but news traveled slower in those days, so what are you going to do?

After the war Lafitte moved his base of operations to Galveston, Texas, and went back into business, playing both sides of the street until driven out by the U.S. government. The two brothers sailed away into legend. While both are said to have continued piracy on the Spanish Main, there is no reliable record of their activities or deaths.

Ching Yih and Ching Yih Saoa – Of all the tales of pirate lore we've ever heard, the most remarkable is that of Ching Yih and his wife, Ching Yih Saoa. Operating in the South China Sea in the early 19th century, Ching Yih came to command a fleet of more than 600 junks and raided the shipping of the rich Chinese mandarins at will. His fleet – divided into six squadrons, each flying a colored pennant for identification – rivaled the strength of the Imperial Navy. Coastal cities that dared to refuse making payments to Ching Yih were ruthlessly destroyed, their citizens slaughtered.

Ching Yih died in a typhoon in 1807. His widow, Ching Yih Saoa, took over, and if anything, was even more ruthless and more successful. She expanded the fleet to more than 800 large junks, thousands of smaller ones, and more than 70,000 men and women. The women were reputed to fight as savagely as the men.

The Chinese navy tried repeatedly to destroy the pirate queen, but Ching Yih Saoa maintained her vicious stranglehold on the South China Sea. Even after the British Royal Navy joined in the fight, the Chinese pirates were uncontrollable. Ching Yih Saoa eventually accepted a pardon from the frustrated Chinese government and retired to a life of luxury with the huge fortune she had amassed.

Barbarossa – The terror of the Mediterranean, Barbarossa was actually two men – Greek-born Turkish brothers who terrorized the coasts of Spain, Italy and Greece during the 16th century. The first Barbarossa (the word means red beard), the elder brother Arouj, came to prominence by capturing two treasure galleys belonging to the pope. Eventually he became ruler of Algiers, but his behavior as a head of state was not notably more temperate than it had been as a pirate, and his subjects appealed for help from the king of Spain. Arouj died in battle with the Spanish in 1518. His younger brother, Khidr, took over the family business - being Barbarossa - and made a better job if it. He took the title of Khair ed-Din, and, swearing allegiance to the sultan of Turkey, was given the post of governor general of Algiers. From that vantage point he became the undisputed ruler of the Barbary Coast, the African shore of the Mediterranean. Hardly a ship passed without his say-so, and Christian shipping was pillaged unmercifully, its treasure looted and its crews sold into slavery at the oars of Barbarossa's galleys. The younger Barbarossa eventually passed from piracy to the somewhat more legitimate role of admiral of the Sultan's fleets, although piracy still played a big part in the job. Unlike his brother, he did most of his work on shore, directing the activities of his fleet from Algiers and later from Constantinople, where he died peacefully in 1546.

Stede Bonnet, the worst pirate ever: Stede Bonnet had a nagging wife. This is not a commentary, just a statement of fact. She was, empirically, a nagging, brutish she-devil of a woman who made his life with her a living, burning, sulfurous tormenting hell. Today, men go to their garage, or workshop, or local bar to escape the ravages of connubial misfortune. But Stede, poor, sad unfortunate Stede, had to get farther away.

His neighbors and family assumed he had lost his mind. Maybe he had. Stede Bonnet was a rich, retired army officer and sugar plantation owner. How but a sudden loss of sanity to else to explain the pathetic course his last year took?

He bought a sloop, named it the Revenge, paid a crew of

other hen-pecked miscreants and low-lifes, and set out for a life of piracy. You have to understand – this just wasn't the way it was supposed to be done. Pirates captured their ships, they didn't buy them. And they didn't hire a crew, they signed agreements for a share of the booty. Stede clearly wasn't cut out for the life he chose. He lacked Pirattitude.

The year was 1718 and piracy was all the rage! If a person set out to build a life as a rock star, one might find a role model – say, Ozzy Osbourne, Ted Nugent or even Mick Jagger. But if you wanted to be a PIRATE, there was only one pirate rock star to worth emulating in 1718 – Edward "Blackbeard" Teach! Finding Blackbeard wasn't the hard part – he could easily find YOU. "Getting rid" of Blackbeard was a bit trickier.

Stede was enamored of his hero. But once he was aboard Blackbeard's ship, Queen Anne's Revenge, he saw what a REAL pirate was like.

In short order Blackbeard figured out that Bonnet knew nothing of seamanship or piracy, so he politely commandeered Stede's ship and "invited" him to stay aboard the Queen Anne's Revenge as a "guest" – a simpering, knee-shaking, urine-soaked blubbering wimp of a guest. When Blackbeard was done with Stede, he gave Bonnet back his ship and sailed away. An enraged Bonnet gave chase in the same way the fat kid who is just learning how to roller-skate chases the ice cream truck.

So, he sailed into Cape Fear and intimidated some fishing boats and robbed lovers in their canoes before being captured in September of - yes, 1718.

Stede Bonnet was tried and convicted of piracy and sentenced to hang one month hence. His impassioned, tear-stained letter to the Governor was of no use. He was hung in

December of that year, just 10 months after he set sail for adventure. They left his body hanging for four days.

Henry Morgan – You figure a pirate has to be pretty good to get a rum named after him; Henry Morgan was the king of 'em all. In the late 17th Century, Morgan was the top of the heap, the never-crowned king of Jamaica. Morgan earned fame and respect among his friends and enemies alike thanks to his dominance of the Caribbean. Not only was he acknowledged as the leader of all the pirates sailing out of Jamaica, he was also for a time simultaneously the English vice admiral charged with cleaning out the pirates, which is certainly good for job security. In his dual role Henry Morgan became the terror of all Spaniards in the West Indies.

He made several legendary attacks on fortified Spanish colonies in the New World, the most famous being his audacious raid on Maracaibo, a city on the coast of Venezuela, during which he and his eight ships and 650 buccaneers sacked two cities, took more than 50,000 English pounds in booty, and routed three Spanish men-o-war. On another raid he took 2,000 pirates on 36 ships for an attack on Panama, routing both a 600-man squadron of cavalry and withstanding a stampede of 2,000 Spanish bulls to capture prizes worth more than 100,000 pounds. Unfortunately, at that point England and Spain were no longer at war, and Morgan was recalled to England and thrown into prison.

But instead of executing Morgan for piracy, Charles II was so impressed with his tales of derring-do that the monarch knighted him and sent him back to Jamaica as lieutenant governor of the island to rid the Caribbean of pirates. And Morgan was as good as his word. When he died in 1688, there were almost no buccaneers left.

Francis Drake – OK, so the renowned English sailor/explorer/adventurer was a privateer, not a pirate. Try telling that to the Spanish. Drake, who was knighted by Queen Elizabeth for his seafaring exploits against the Spanish, was the most resolute, domineering and amazing figure in the history of the sea. He rose from humble origins to be the greatest admiral and seaman of his age.

After one spectacularly successful raid down the Spanish Main, Drake took his ship, the Golden Hind, around the tip of South America and up the Pacific coast at least as far north as San Francisco, possibly as far as Oregon. Believing the Spanish would be lying in wait for him if he retraced his route, he headed out across the uncharted Pacific, finally making it back to England almost three years after departing, bringing tales of amazing adventures and an enormous treasure in Spanish loot. That made him the first English captain to circumnavigate the globe. You could even argue that he was the first captain to achieve the feat – Magellan, after all, got himself killed in the Philippines, so why people credit him with being the first to sail around the world is a mystery to us.

King Philip of Spain was itching to punish England, and began assembling a huge fleet for the expedition. Drake's most important work in defeating the Armada was actually accomplished the summer before Philip's fleet sailed. Raiding the coast of Spain, he harried the Spanish preparations and destroyed many of the supplies being assembled for the venture, not the least of which were thousands of seasoned barrel staves meant to hold the supplies of the fleet. The following year, when the Armada sailed, sailors found spoiled meat and rancid water in the green barrels. In truth, the Armada never had much of a chance; even Philip was confidently counting on a miracle. Under Drake's command, the British fleet harried the Armada up the English Channel. The Spanish admiral never offered full battle, and the British were eventually able to scatter his ships to the north, where the winds and storms of the North Sea and the Atlantic Ocean did most of the work of destroying the doomed fleet.

Drake, alas, died somewhat ignominiously, of dysentery in 1596, and was buried at sea. Still, his is the image of the dauntless sea dog, the avenging mariner defying the whole fleet of the Spanish Empire with a smile and an insouciant bounce. If there hadn't been a Francis Drake, we dare say there couldn't have been an Errol Flynn.

Jose Gaspar – The best thing about Jose Gaspar, also known as Gasparilla, is that he almost certainly didn't exist. According to Dana Groffe Jr., a "senior gunner of Ye Mystic Crew of Gasparilla," (about which more in a moment) the sole proof of the myth was the word of an old salt named Juan Gomez, more than 100 years old, who claimed to have been Gasparilla's cabin boy back in the good old days.

Jose Gaspar is reputed to have been a Spanish noble and naval officer, a fierce, intelligent combatant and a real ladies' man. He wooed widely and well, which got him into hot water. One of his spurned lovers cooked up a story about him planning to steal the crown jewels. He fled before he could be arrested and, with a band of cutthroats, hijacked the Spanish galleon Floridablanca (white flower) in 1783 and took to a life of piracy.

For the next 38 years, Gasparilla attacked merchant ships from all countries. By some accounts, he plundered more than 400 ships. Even Gasparilla's death is the stuff of legend. In 1821 he chose to retire at the age of 65, a rare mark for a man in his dangerous profession. But as he was getting ready to divide the loot of almost 40 years of piracy, he spotted what appeared to be a helpless British merchantman and gave chase. Alas! It was a trap! As he got into range, the ship dropped the Union Jack and raised the Stars and Stripes, revealing itself as U.S.S. Enterprise of the American Navy. Dozens of cannon roared out from the battleship, and the Floridablanca was quickly overcome.

Spurning capture, Jose Gaspar climbed to the bow of his ship and yelled, "Gasparilla dies by his own hand, not the enemy's." He wrapped the anchor's chain around his waist and, with cutlass held high over his head, jumped into the dark waters and disappeared below the waves. The life of Jose Gaspar was over – if it had ever actually started.

A small, hand-picked group of his crew had witnessed the battle from shore, where they were guarding the treasure. They loaded their booty into the longboat and rowed up the Peace River, where they buried their treasure and left. They were never seen again and the treasure was never found. Which means, to the romantic among us, that it's still out there somewhere, waiting to be discovered.

Jose Gaspar's story – whether history or myth – lives on today in the city of Tampa's Gasparilla Festival, sort of the Florida version of Mardi Gras. The cream of Tampa society, organized as The Mystic Crew of Gasparilla, re-enact the invasion of the town – an event that probably never happened, led by a man who probably didn't exist.

And the best part is, no actual persons were harmed in the making of the legend. Probably.

Calico Jack Rackham – We like the name Calico Jack more than we like the pirate himself. It's one of the great names of piratedom. As you will read below when reviewing the career of Anne Bonney, Jack wasn't the bravest pirate to ever sail the seas. When his ship was cornered by the British, Jack and his crew hid below decks while the two women aboard, Anne and Mary Read, fought the boarders, calling scornfully to the pirates below to come up and fight like men. But what he lacked in gumption, Calico Jack made up for in style. His nickname came from his habit of wearing a coat and trousers of that material.

Rackham sailed out of the pirate colony of New Providence in the early 18th century, preying on shipping from the Spanish Main and the American colonies. When the British sent a fleet under the new governor of the Bahamas to suppress the buccaneers, Rackham was one of those who accepted amnesty in exchange for giving up the trade. But he quickly spent the remainder of his money and went back to sea to "earn" his living the only way he knew how. He was hunted down by the British and executed. His only real claim to fame is his association with the female pirate Anne Bonney and her famous last words to him. But he had a great name, didn't he?

Anne Bonney and Mary Read – Anne was a rich girl who grew up in Charles Town, South Carolina. She had a streak of wildness in her and went to sea, marrying James Bonney, a deserter from the Royal Navy and now a pirate captain. But she wasn't that easily satisfied and later took as a lover an up-and-coming pirate named "Calico Jack" Rackham. What Jack lacked in "testicular fortitude," Anne had in double dosage. When there was fighting to be done, Anne wore the pants and Jack hit the rack.

Mary was aboard Jack's ship disguised as a man and going by the name Mark Read when she caught Anne's wicked wandering eye. Mary was herself married to a pirate, one Tom Deane. Like Anne, Mary apparently was the braver, tougher member of the union. According to legend, Tom was once challenged by another pirate. Mary, fearing for his life, fought the man herself and killed him.

No love affair was ever documented between the lady pirates, who were reputed to be "just good friends," nor has there ever been any serious suggestion of it by historians. But for the love of Blackbeard's ghost, we think their story would be much more interesting (and marketable) if they were lovers. So, we now give our reader a moment to imagine such a relationship ... Are you done? Not quite? That's all right, we'll wait. Aaahh.

All right, moving on. When the pirate hunter Captain Barnet caught up with Rackham's ship, Anne and Mary were the only members of the crew (including Calico Jack himself) who put up much of a fight. While the pirates skulked below, Anne and Mary tried to fight off the entire crew of the British ship.

Anne and Mary stood trial with the rest of the crew, but "pleaded their bellies" (that is, claimed they were pregnant) and were spared the hempen dance. Anne was allowed to see Jack before his execution. She told him – and these are the best, most macho words we have ever heard of a woman saying to a man – "Jack, if you had fought like a man, you wouldn't be hanging like a dog." There is no record of his response, but we can't imagine it helped his mood.

Mary died later that year in prison. Anne disappeared from piracy and history. No births were ever recorded.

Chapter 9
Great pirates of the screen

We don't want to leave the subject of past pirates without paying homage to a few of the scurvy sea dogs who have inspired us and other scalawags into occasionally spouting this piratical gibberish.

Two we will NOT be honoring are: The Dread Pirate Roberts, from "The Princess Bride," and Gene Kelly from "The Pirate." Don't get us wrong. We enjoyed "The Princess Bride" as much as anyone. It's a great date movie. And Gene Kelly is the manliest dancer this or any other country has ever produced. But the Dread Pirate Roberts talked in a sissy English accent, not a strong, burred, Cornish grunt, and as manly as Gene was, he was still a dancer, and "The Pirate" was full of capering, which is not our favorite art form. Even when Gene is doing the capering.

So here are a few of the pirate figures who made us what we are today.

Long John Silver – There have been several portrayals

of this rogue, but our favorite would have to be Robert Newton – the patron saint of International Talk Like a Pirate Day – from the 1950 Disney version of "Treasure Island." Newton is often credited with creating the common perception of what pirates sound like. He was from Cornwall, and the growls and inflections were his natural speaking patterns. So don't let lubbers tell you pirates talk with a Cockney accent – Cockney! Don't be absurd. It's Cornish, thanks to Robert Newton.

Two other great Long Johns were:

• Wallace Beery in the 1934 version. He was a terrific rascally rogue.

• Tim Curry in "Muppet Treasure Island." Yes, we know. Muppets, songs, the transvestite from "Rocky Horror Picture Show," even a little capering. But Curry goes so far over the top in this movie that he's absolutely hilarious. This is not a scary pirate. This is a guy's guy, just having fun being a pirate, and a peg-legged one at that.

And while we're on the subject, let's agree right here and now that "Treasure Island" by Robert Louis Stevenson is the greatest pirate story ever written. Adventure, excitement, bravery. It's a story that captures the hearts and minds of youngsters and can continue to hold them into adulthood. According to the Internet Movie Database there were 12 screen or TV versions of this classic – the best was probably the 1934 Wallace Beery version – and more than 30 movies with some variant, of "Treasure Island" in the title, including the 1939 "Charlie Chan on Treasure Island," which we have no interest in seeing.

Captain Jack Sparrow in "Pirates of the Caribbean – The Curse of the Black Pearl." This Disney film brought the pirate movie back to the forefront of the cinema in 2003 (well, we like to think we had a little to do with priming the public for it, too) and most notable was Johnny Depp's Oscar-nominated performance as Jack Sparrow. Sure, Orlando Bloom was as adorable as ever, making the teen girls giggle and swoon, and Geoffrey Rush's sinister Barbossa was devilishly delicious, but the center of the picture was Captain Jack. While Depp credits the legendary Rolling Stones guitarist Keith Richards as the inspiration for the characterization, credit must also be given to Sparrow's archnemesis in the story – no, not Barbossa and not the naval commander fellow played adequately enough by some English actor who's name we didn't bother to look up. Jack Sparrow's biggest foe was gravity herself. Jack seemed to be in a life-or-death struggle throughout with that natural force, as he listed at impossible angles throughout the movie. Ships sink beneath him, things fall on top of him or just beyond his reach, and he just keeps coming back for more. Finally, however, he is able to use his gravity to his advantage (as in judo, turning your opponent's strength against him) as he leaps to freedom from the fort's stone walls. He is, at the heart of things, a triumph of man over nature.

Captain Hook – This is one of the first pirates most of us ever saw, in "Peter Pan." Either the Disney classic, which is a wonderful movie except for that whole Red Man thing that is so unapologetically racist that it's embarrassing to watch, or the stage version starring Mary Martin that played over and over again when we were kids. Captain Hook was evil, all right, he even had a hook! And yet he managed to never actually frighten the kids who were watching. A fairly neat trick.

Geena Davis as pirate captain **Morgana Adams in "Cutthroat Island"** – Yes, we can hear you now. "But wait, Geena Davis is ... a girl!" Yes, she is. And a damn fine one at that. One who proved you can have good legs and still sack and pillage with the best of 'em. Aye, she's one wench who could join our crew any day. We can also hear you coughing politely and pointing out that, Geena's finer points aside, "Cutthroat Island" is not a particularly good movie. No, sadly, it pretty much bites. But Geena is fine in it. She's a salty wench and swashbuckles with the best of them.

Gabriel Byrne in the 1990 "Shipwrecked," which also goes by the name "Hakon Hakonsen," a Norwegian movie about a boy who signs aboard a ship as a cabin boy and discovers real pirates. Byrne plays the malevolent pirate John Merrick, possibly the most evil pirate in a kids' pirate movie. He's actually pretty scary.

Errol Flynn – In "Captain Blood" and again in "The Sea Hawk" (they were virtually the same movie, they even used some of the same footage), Errol Flynn was probably the greatest cinema pirate ever. In fact, forget the probably. He was. Hell, he was playing a pirate even in movies that had nothing to do with pirates and were shot in the desert. He just had that way – the smile, the bounce, the Pirattitude. Now, somewhere out there someone is spitting his warm milk and saying, "Wait, in those movies he was a privateer, not a pirate." Well, excuse us. The distinction is that privateers were sanctioned by the crown to prey on enemy shipping, no questions asked, and they shared their booty with the government and any private investors. Pirates, on the other hand, were, shall we say, in business for themselves. This commitment to private enterprise, to entrepreneurship, if you will, should be commended. But that's neither here nor there. The point is, Errol Flynn was the man. He was it.

Chapter 10

The Official Talk Like A Pirate Personality Inventory (TOTLAPPI)

Are ye the talk of the dock? Cock of the walk? Rank of the plank? Do the mates want to be like you and the beauties want to be with you? Or are ye a fine example of piratical womanliness?

Now that we've learned a little something about some of the real and fictional characters who make up pirate lore, it's time to find out just where YOU fall in the ranks of piracy. This little personality test will tell ye and everyone else just what kind of bucko (or buckette, as the case may be) you are and are meant to be. After you have answered the questions and tallied up yer scores, there are specific "characters" of whose ilk ye may also be. Answer the questions in truth and we'll not scuttle your tub. Lie and may the sharks give ye quarter, for Davey Jones knows we won't.

IMPORTANT NOTE: School psychologists, social workers and

clinicians should be wary of using the TOTLAPPI when qualifying students for IDEA services, DSM IV identifications (under any axis) or as a part of any professional assessment. Medical professionals are hereby cautioned not to use the TOTLAPPI as a tool to determine appropriate medications and/or dosage. Lawyers are hereby notified that the results of the TOTLAPPI are not admissible in most state and federal courts with the exceptions of those in the Bahamas, French New Guinea, Madagascar and Wyoming. Amnesty International has requested a moratorium on the TOTLAPPI in death penalty cases until the American College of Psychiatry and the British Psychological Association can complete a twelve-year longitudinal study into the TOTLAPPI's efficacy rate and cultural bias. This tool was designed for use solely by pirate captains and Web surfers. Please do not attempt this in any professional setting.

Grub and grog

1. After a busy day of smiting pirates with a belaying pin, I can be counted on to wash down the taste of my domination with:

(a) rum, straight from the bung hole while the lads raise the barrel over my reclining form.

(b) a tankard or two – or six – of cold ale. And leave me alone!

(c) saltwater with a urine chaser. No ice.

(d) a nice Barbera D'Alba from Italy. Four or five years old and allowed to breathe for ten minutes before it ever TOUCHES crystal.

2. Lashing captives to the mizzenmast is hard work and makes any pirate hunger something fierce. The only thing that will quell this buccaneer's belly would have to be:

(a) a slab of sperm whale, fresh from the whale's belly,

roasted over a hot cannon.

(b) hardtack. Easy on the boll weevils. And salted meat with a tankard of ale or seven.

(c) whatever is in the chumbucket ... or spilled off the captain's table.

(d) swordfish in a lime baste garnished with parsley, red potatoes and baby onions.

Fightin'!

3) Maintaining discipline on board is:

(a) fun because there are so many ways to inflict pain ... ah, the choices!

(b) important to the orderly operation of the vessel, and a great spectator sport.

(c) the only way ye'll get me to wash off the first few layers o' filth.

(d) necessary, but can be messy and sometimes leaves a mark.

4. When locked in fierce combat with an evenly matched foe, my weapon of choice is:

(a) pistols! As long as the other pirate has a belaying pin.

(b) cutlass and dagger with another dagger clenched in my teeth for added "daggerosity."

(c) chumbucket and chamber pot with another chumbucket clenched in my teeth for added "chumbucketosity."

(d) my witty repartee and cutting fashion comments.

5. I learned to fight:

(a) by punching slabs of meat in the galley until the cook tried to throw me out and I beat him soundly with my fists and forehead!

(b) when I was tied into a bag of feral cats and thrown off a bridge. First one out got to survive.

(c) with all the other little guttersnipes over tasty bits of slime in the gutter. Arrr, I miss my family.

(d) in Paris, under the strict tutelage of the Marquis d' Salami, master of the parry and thrust!

6. Fighting is:

(a) an excuse to use me cannon. BOOM! I love it!

(b) sometimes necessary and always fun.

(c) what we do when somebody has moved me chum bucket.

(d) fabulous aerobic exercise.

7. The nastiest scrape I was ever in ended when:

(a) me hook got stuck in a man's skull and I had to lop off his head in order to continue the battle. Well, ye should have seen the terrified looks on the scurvy dogs' faces when they realized I was pummeling them with their own captain's head!

(b) I lopped off this pirate's head and he took about six or seven steps with his arms waving in front of him as if he wanted to say, "Hey! Where's my head." To top it off, there was no way he would ever find his head because it had landed in the chumbucket.

(c) me opponent went to gouge out me eye and realized he was sticking his thumb through me patch into me empty eye socket! I laughed and shouted, "Too Late!" The look on his face was priceless!

(d) I stuck my thumb into what I thought was my

opponent's eye. Turned out, it was just a patch covering his empty eye socket! He laughed and said, "Too Late!" But he did it in a way that was just adorable!

Loving

8. The first thing I do when we get into port is:
(a) grab the sauciest wenches (or, for women, the studliest sailors) in the pub and kiss 'em like they've never been kissed. Then, I drink enough to forget they've had more pirates (or strumpets) than baths.
(b) I size up a potential lover, then, I drink them under a table and leave them with nothin' but a foggy memory of somebody putting their pinky and thumb to their ear and mouth saying, "call me."
(c) gargle with fresh urine and give me tooth a good brushing.
(d) check the latest dispatches from Paris to see what the Dauphin is wearing and where I can find ruffles like those!

9. Those long, lonely nights at sea I find that I:
(a) need to be careful to remember which is the hand and which is the hook.
(b) have developed an immunity to a jellyfish's sting. Mmm, I calls this jellyfish "Sweet Betty."
(c) I'm sorry. What was the question?
(d) transport myself into ANY French bordello simply by lighting a few candles, breathing in the salt air and letting the caress of the ocean waves bring me to perfect carnal bliss.

Treasure

10. To my way of thinking, the perfect treasure would be:

(a) GOLD, fool! More gold than I can imagine! And when I CAN imagine it, I find out that there is MORE GOLD! Arrr! It's like I'm crapping GOLD!

(b) waking up on the morning of my seventy-second birthday realizing that I have no regrets for the things I have done, only for the things I haven't, and that a life of adventure has been the "real" treasure.

(c) a solid, stainless pewter chumbucket with a fancy copper ladle. Just like a gentleman's gentleman would have.

(d) silks from China, china from Italy, French lace and Irish linen. A veritable United Nations of plunder!

SCORING – Give yourself 5 points for every (a) you answered, 3 points for every (b), two points for every (c) and 1 point for every (d). Now add them up.

Now, me matey's, here's what your scoring means.

If you scored between 1-9 you are
A COMPLETE MORON
Go back and answer the question you missed. Arrr! If I had a plank here right now!!!

If you scored between 10-15 you may consider yourself:
LORD or LADY PERCIVAL FIDDLE-FADDLE
Thanks for your interest in joining our crew, but we're afraid we have no suitable openings at this time. You are a gentleman/gentlewoman – or possibly a gentleman's gentleman or a gentlewoman's gentlewoman. Whichever, you

are perhaps a little TOO gentle to be happy on a pirate ship, and might find more satisfaction as – oh, say, assistant purser on the Love Boat. You like the finer things in life, not that there's anything WRONG with that, but if you're forced to spend a lot of time in the company of a pirate crew, it's probably not going to be a fun time for any of you, at least not until the captain decides it's time for the floggings, in which case at least HE'S likely to have a good time. Which is not to say that you can't strike terror into the hearts of your prey on the open seas. Any merchantman who finds himself paired against you in combat knows he's in for a good sassing.

If you scored between 15-25, you are:
SLOPPY DENNIS/DENISE PUSSBUCKET
You look old for your age. You've heard about hygiene, but to you it's just that thing that happens to other pirates. You like what you like. People think of you as a blight on humanity, a carbuncle on the alabaster skin of mankind. You wallow in the reek of the bilge with the other rats. It's a nice fit, but the Board of Health wants to have a few words with you. Still, every pirate crew needs a few people who are not only willing to take on the dirty jobs, but will actually line up to volunteer for them. You're not above cheating, but to your way of thinking, that's just playing the game better than anyone else.

If you scored between 25-40, you are:
BOSUN SECOND CLASS JERRY/JENNY JONES
A born leader needs a whole herd – er, we mean crew – of born followers, and that's where you come in. You have taken timidity, labeled it efficiency, and made it your calling card. Do you remember the last time you took a chance? Creativity is

not your strong suit. You are good at doing what you are told to do and that, in itself, is a gift. It's not a gift to you, mind you, but rather a gift to those who will be there to tell you what to do.

If you scored between 40-45, you are:

SICK SAMMY/SAMANTHA O'BEACH

You are a pirate on the go, and anyone ahead of you had better watch his back. We hope you never find out where we live. You are violent and crude – a dangerous combination in any century but on a pirate ship you are a captain's best friend and his worst nightmare. You are capable of great leadership and unspeakable personal habits. You are the embodiment of chaos and body odor. Grandmothers frighten children with stories about you. *Your* grandmother. *Your* children! Fortunately, your ten word vocabulary does not include ambition. If you had even the slightest clue where you were going, men and women would follow you. As it is, it is enough that they know where you are and can distract you by throwing bright shiny objects on the deck to steer you away from their path.

If you scored between 45-50, you are:

CAP'N DEVILISH DAN/DANITA SMACKBOTTOM

Some men and women are born great, some achieve greatness and some slit the throats of any scallawag who stands between them and the mantle of power. You are a born leader – whether anyone is following is immaterial. Not that mindless violence is the only avenue open to you – but why take an avenue when you have complete freeway access? You are the definitive man of action. Your buckle was swashed long ago and you have never been so sure of anything in your life as in your ability to bend everyone to your will. You will call anyone out and cut off their head if they show any sign of taking you on or backing down. You cannot be saddled with tedious underlings, but if one of your lieutenants shows an overly developed sense of ambition he may find more suitable accommodations in Davy Jones' locker. That is, of course, IF you notice him. You tend to be self absorbed – a weakness that may keep you from seeing enemies where they are and imagining them where they are not.

Chapter 11

Slapshots: Culled from the Files of "Ask Cap'n Slappy"

He's a legendary figure, envied and admired by men, desired by women, idolized by children. At least in his dreams. He's Cap'n Slappy, the sage of the Seven Seas and master of the dread pirate ship The Festering Boil.

When we launched our Web site, www.talklikeapirate.com, we thought it would be funny to have an "advice" column. As with so many things we thought would be funny, no one with sounder judgment was around to dissuade us, so we did it. Mark, in his pirate persona, started "Ask Cap'n Slappy." It's pretty much exactly like "Dear Abby," if Abby were a seriously irresponsible guy who enjoys beer, belching and a good fight, and who loathes personal relationships that last longer than 15 minutes. We invited readers to send in questions on any subject, because Slappy was equally qualified in all fields (which is to say, not at all). And we promised right up front that all responses would be 100 percent alcohol-fueled. We figured this would be helpful to anyone who wasn't sure whether to actually follow his advice.

Well, the response was way beyond our greatest hopes, or Slappy's wildest fear. Much to our surprise, "Ask Cap'n Slappy" has turned out to be the most popular part of this whole venture. So, with no further ado than to remind to send your questions to capnslappy@talklikeapirate.com, we give you a little touch of Slappy in the night.

Dear Cap'n Slappy,

Why are 16 men on a dead man's chest? And what's the deal with the bottle of rum, anyway? Are they drinking it? Or did it kill the poor guy who now has 16 men on his chest? What gives here, Cap'n? **Edmund Fitzgerald**

Dear Fitz,

The lyrics to this popular pirate tune have always been unsettling to me as well. For one thing, there is no way that sixteen pirate asses could fit on a dead man's chest. The seating space, even for a very large chest and very small asses, would accommodate only four ... maybe five. But let's say that the pirates are standing on the chest. With a one-footed group stand while they held other pirates on their shoulders, you could conceivably get sixteen pirates stacked on the man's chest. This would explain him being dead. The bottle of rum might have led to the man saying, "Hey, you sixteen pirates! I bet you can't all stand on my chest at once!" The answer to, "what gives?" would be, "Clearly, his sternum."

Cap'n Slappy

Dear Cap'n Slappy,

Do you have to have a parrot to be a pirate or talk like one?? **Anon**

Ahoy Parrot-head!

It's Talk Like a Pirate Day, NOT Talk Like a Parrot Day! The parrot is as much a part of Talk Like a Pirate Day as it would be at a Jimmy Buffet concert. Nice set dressing, but it doesn't make the songs any sweeter! The best parrots are the "stuffed/dead" ones. Unless you like to dress in newsprint.

Could you imagine Talk Like a Parrot Day? People would be gutting each other in the streets. "STOP REPEATING WHAT I SAY IN THAT HIGH NASAL VOICE! YOU #*#@($)#@!!!" people would say just before slitting you open with their cutlass.

Now, if you have a parrot, that's great! Treat them with care and they will be great gifts for your great-grandchildren, but for the love of Neptune, leave them in their cages on September 19th. And for Jimmy's sake, don't take them to the concert!

Cap'n Slappy

Dear Cap'n Slappy,

How do you spell savy? **Bloody Mary Bonnie**

Ahoy Bloody Mary!

Spelling is hard. Nobody knows that like Ol' Cap'n Slappy. Fortunately for you, I have created a mnemonic device to help me remember how to spell "S-A-V-V-Y." It's sung to the tune of "L-O-V-E" (a tune your mother would know).

It goes a little something like this:

S is for the way you SASS my way!
A is for the ASS I kicked today!

V and V are VERY, VERY,
stuck on how you're scary
Y is for your YAP that's flappin'
cuz ye won't shut yer trap and
SAVVY is just how bright you seem to me.
SAVVY an understanding wench, ye be.
Our love stands the measure
You know you're my buried treasure
SAVVY is why you've chosen me!
I hope this helps, me Bonny, Bloody Lass!
Cap'n Slappy

Dear Cap'n Slappy,
What do port and starboard mean? **LaJaynes H. Dupuy**

Ahoy LaJaynes!
If ye be standing on a ship (or a boat) and looking toward the bow (the "pointy-pointy" part), then "port" would be on your left side and "starboard" would be on your right. To your back is the "stern" or the "poop." And for all of ye lubbers out thar what don't know ... All that greenish-bluish-grey, bouncy stuff around the boat be "water." Now, take your seasick pills.
Cap'n Slappy

Dear Cap'n Slappy,
Which do you prefer, Cap'n, lootin' or plunderin'? **Cap'n McPitterPat**

Arrr! Good Question, Cap'n McPitterPat!
Some days I feels like lootin'. Some days I feels like plunderin'. Some days I feels like beating someone senseless with me fists and forehead. And some days I just feels "not so fresh."

But ne'er a day goes by that I don't feel like getting blistering drunk and playing "Full Contact Scrabble!" Thar be a triple word score and a belayin' pin to the noggin here fer all!
Cap'n Slappy

Ahoy, Cap'n!
What be yer professional advice on namin' me ship? **Mad Cap'n (t' be) Amy o' the ???**

Dear Cap'n Amy
The secret to a good ship name be in findin' the right chord to strike fear and/or nausea into yer enemy. I likes the names what look like they be goin' one way and end up goin' t'another. Startin' with a word like "Golden" one gets the idea of something very nice and expensive-like. But if ye follow it up with something as repulsive as "Nasal Polyp" then ye have somethin' else altogether.
Arrr! The Golden Nasal Polyp be a great name fer a ship!
Cap'n Slappy

Ahoy thar Slappy!
I've got a question fer ye that I need answered smartly. Fer Halloween this year I'm goin' as a pirate. I was wonderin' what kinda things I'm going to need to be successful and look me best. I already have one o' them eye patches so that I can say I was thrown overboard in a mutiny and saved meself from the eye-bitin sharks. I also have a pirate hat and a fake gray beard like those I think me pirate role models would have worn when they shaved for a beautiful lass but didn't want to tell their mates. But what else do I need to complete me costume? I need to look good fer me lasses. Arrr. **Yer loyal reader and shipmate**

Aye, Loyal Reader!

It be about time for "Cap'n Slappy's Pirate Paraphernalia Checklist:"

___ Eyepatch? – Check

___ Pirate Hat and/or Bandanna – Check

___ Fake Grey Beard or Black Beard with Burning Wicks (optional) – Check

___ Peg Leg with realistic "clomp, clomp" sound – Still need

___ Hook (partly rusty) – a "must"

___ Real or Plastic Parrot

___ Greatcoat what stinks of twenty years of dried blood and salt water – ewww!

___ Gold Doubloons to flash around – go to bank for Sacajawea Dollars

___ Blousy Shirt – borrow from Mom

___ Nasty-dirty trousers – borrow from Dad

___ Big Leather Boots – ???

___ Big Leather Boots – ???!!!

___ Big Leather BOOTS!!! – Awe, hell, just wear some Nikes and tell everyone ye be a cross-trainin' pirate.

And that's about all ye need. If ye be plannin' on dancin' or drinkin' leave yer sword at home ... we want the date to last for the evenin' now, don't we?

Cap'n Slappy

Ahoy, Matey!

How do you even be a pirate? Will you be my Cap'n? Pirates are very awesome - I wish I could be one! Do you shoot whales? Do you catch fish? Do you try to shoot dolphins? **Good-bye, Miss Emily**

P.S. - I am 6 years old.

Ahoy Miss Emily!
There are some things in life you become just by saying you are and then acting like you are. "Friends" is one. "Good Student" is another. "Pirate" can be kind of like that, too.

But Cap'n Slappy is more of a "Pirate-Guy." And while I do catch fish, I don't shoot whales or dolphins. Cap'n Slappy likes to eat fish, and he likes to look at whales and dolphins. So, no shooting whales, dolphins or people!

And before you read ANYTHING else on this Web site, you should have your mommy or daddy take a good look at it. (Most of what we have here is for adults and MUCH older kids).

Thank you for writing! (You write better than most of the adults who write to Cap'n Slappy!)
Cap'n Slappy

Dear Cap'n Slappy,
Ever since my girlfriend came back from Iraq, she's had this funny smell about her. It wasn't the war. She was there in 1987, traveling with a touring all-star roller derby team, and that camel smell just won't go away. My question is, "Can I deduct the cost of her leotards on my taxes?" **Frugal in Tulsa**

Dear Tight with Tights,
Your girlfriend sounds so sexy. When you say "funny" smell, are we talking about "funny/humorous" or "funny/sweet-baby-Jesus-what-is-that?" If your answer is, "funny/humorous," leotard cleaning is not deductible. If your answer is, "funny/sweet-baby-Jesus-what-is-that?" you may file a 1241-b.o. unless you live in Oklahoma, which you do. Under the circumstances, you owe Cap'n Slappy $55.24 and a case of gin. Please send cash or money order along with your girlfriend and I will consider your debt paid in full.
Cap'n Slappy

Dear Cap'n Slappy,

Last night I was out clubbing with my homies when I met an unsavory ill-kempt bearded man with a wooden leg. As hot as he was I turned down an invitation to go submarine watching from the fo'c's'le. Now I am having second thoughts. Do you think I have missed my chance for true love? **Wench Wannabe**

Dear Wenchabe,

The great thing about missing your chance for true love is that you are always left with a second chance at false sex. If an ill-kempt man with a pegleg and a beard isn't your style, may I suggest any number of tuba players or slack-jawed pig farmers? These fellows will fit in fine with your homies and next thing you know, they are just part of the posse. In the meantime, lay off the "Oprah." She's got you thinking mad thoughts.

Cap'n Slappy

Dear Cap'n Slappy,

How long are leeches good for? Please respond quickly! **Dying to Know**

Dear Dying,

It depends on what you want them for. I enjoy mine pickled in urine and served with a side dish of Chum. Do you have refrigeration? Or at least indoor plumbing?

Cap'n Slappy

Dear Slappy,

I heard ye are a real doctor. Can ye help me? My mum is

always tellin' me I'm too fat. I think I'm fine, but now I don't know. I'm only about 40 pounds overweight and I have large breasts to match me curvy hips. Is me mum right? **Chesty**

Dear Chesty,

I AM a real doctor and am recognized as such in countries that aren't so picky about how a person becomes a doctor. Cap'n Slappy considers forty pounds overweight a good start. If you have large heaving breasts (Did you say they were heaving? If not, let me add the word "heaving.") and curvy hips, Dr. Cap'n Slappy will certainly want to give you a thorough examination. If your mum also has the heaving breasts, Dr. Cap'n Slappy will also want to look at … arr … I mean … into that, too.

Yours for universal medical care, Cap'n Slappy

O Cap'n!

I once loved a pirate wench. She was a beauty. But our parents came between us. They wanted us to tie the knot, or splice the mainbrace or something like that, and of course that meant we never wanted to see each other again. She sailed on, and is now probably a beautiful and happy wench while I am stuck in dry dock wondering. O Cap'n My Cap'n, whatever become of that buxom beauty? How do I stop thinking of her, or is that impossible? **Red Willy**

My Dear Ruddy Willy,

Your parents were right! She is a saucy wench and you are a man of the sea. Sure, you're dry-docked … as well you should stay. But to stop thinking of her, do like the Cap'n does … drink heavily, sing sad songs at the night sky and play darts. Darts, lad, be the cure for love gone wrong … or just plain gone. But don't forget to drink! It will help with the singin' and make you think you're a better darts shooter than you are.

By the way, your parents have moved on without you, too. Have a nice day.

Back to my bitter dart game, Cap'n Slappy

Any tips on what to do about that "not so fresh" feeling?
Stinky

Ahoy Stinky!

Alright ... don't "ahoy" too close ... stay right there ... WHEW! You weren't kiddin' about that "not so freshness." The Cap'n is nothing if not an expert in the manly art of pirate hygiene. You might say I have a P-H-D (pirate hygiene doctorate) in it! That's just a little joke we like to tell in the Mayo Clinic's Salty Bastards Wing. Here are a few tips that will clear the air and make you just one of the lads.

Step One: Don't do anything that might make you stinky. In other words ... nothing that would make you sweat or smell of sweaty things or fish. No more chum fights, either!

Step Two: Brush your hair one hundred times every night. Cap'n Slappy's ex-wench used to do this and she hardly stunk at all.

Step Four: Skip step three, which was something about "soap and water," and go straight to "blaming other pirates for 'that smell.'"

Step Five: Do something every day that makes the captain keelhaul you! This will accomplish two things: a good barnacle scrub for you, and the ship's hull will receive a nice coating of protective "weasel grease" from your oily hide.

Keep this up, my boy, and you will be "Pirate of the year!"
Cap'n Slappy

Dear Cap/n Slappy,

OK, so I know all about the biology. I understand about vascular constriction and lubrication and sensitivity and all that stuff. I've had the sex ed classes and understand the mechanics. There's just one question I still haven't figured out.

How do you convince her? **Lonely swabbie**

Dear Lone Swabbie,

Have we ruled out your obvious hygiene deficits? If so, there are some simple rules to follow when you are wooing a wench.

Rule 1 – Never appear to be "needy." Wenches will have no respect for a pirate who begs for it. Present an aloof (but fresh smelling) air. Give her the impression that you could do without her or her kind. As a show of your aloofness, kiss a fancy lad full on the mouth and let her see you do it. Nothing screams "come hither" like the woman who thinks ye may fancy the lads a bit too much.

Rule 2 – Get in touch with the comic inside you. Wenches love to laugh. Try walking into the mizzenmast while looking another direction or slipping in chum spillage. Humor is the best knicker-removal system known to man. With the right joke or anecdote, you will have her bloomers under your bunk in no time.

Rule 3 – Above all, act like you've been thar before. This is not something you learn in one of them fancy-schmancy "books" with the charcoal drawings. (although the books are more easily put away when you are done with them). Experience is not nearly so important as the appearance of experience.

But first things first. Get that bath! And would a couple of Botox injections kill you?

Cap'n Slappy

Is it wrong to be a woman with a pirate fetish? And I mean an absolute, 100% "I need a pirate and I need him NOW" pirate fetish? **Jes**

Dear Jes,
Sweet Mother of Pearl!
NO! It is NEVER wrong for a woman to have an absolute 100% "I need a pirate and I need him NOW" pirate fetish! But if you and your friends are concerned about this, I know just the place for you. Have you heard of Cap'n Slappy's Salty Seadog Sanitarium? Our trained staff will indulge your every ... I mean "address" your issues in a thoughtful and professional and "CONFIDENTIAL" manner. Sure, there's a waiting list, but I am sure we can make some arrangements.
Fanning myself with my hook, Cap'n Slappy

Chapter 12

A pirate can dream, can't he?

So here we are at the end of the book, with dreams of glory dancing in our sleepy heads.

Sure, this whole thing is nothing more than a protracted joke. But what if Talk Like a Pirate Day really caught on? Yeah, we've already reached millions. But what if we reached EVERYBODY? What if everyone on the planet put aside their differences for one day a year and began talking like a pirate every September 19th, just for the fun of it? What if this simple, silly action, taken by everybody, created a common sense of playfulness all around the globe, helping people from every country and walk of life realize that the things they have in common are more important than the things that divide them?

Maybe, in the not-so-distant future, you'd see a newspaper story something like this:

Arr! Nobel Peace Prize awarded

OSLO, Norway (AP) – Two Americans were awarded the Nobel Peace Prize yesterday in a ceremony that marked a sharp break with tradition. Instead of solemn speeches in front of an august audience of statesmen and clergy, John "Ol' Chumbucket" Baur and Mark "Cap'n Slappy" Summers received their prize while joking, drinking, burping and nearly rupturing the tense diplomatic relationship between the United States and France.

The Nobel Peace Prize, named for Alfred Nobel, inventor of dynamite, was awarded to Summers and Baur for giving birth to International Talk Like a Pirate Day.

The news two months ago that the two Oregonians had won the prize over such distinguished nominees as French President Jacques Chirac, former American Secretary of State Colin Powell, and beloved Brazilian monkey trainer Hidalgo "Cooter" Vasquez shocked the world. The announcement was widely seen as a "little Norwegian joke" by the selection committee, but it turned out to be true.

The surprise was even greater right from the beginning of the presentation ceremony, when Summers, before taking his seat at the head table, walked over to Norway's Queen Sonja, swept her up in his arms and kissed her deeply. The Queen, now in her 60s, seemed surprised but not offended.

In his introductory speech, their close personal friend, Pulitzer Prize winner Dave Barry, referred to the pair as, "two guys whom I have never met before, but they seem OK so long as you don't get too close to them." Later that evening, Barry remarked that he would now insist on calling them, "my close personal friends, Nobel Peace Prize winners, The Pirate Guys" and afterward, told the delegate from Stockholm a booger joke in Danish.

Summers, who for some reason wore a kilt to the formal occasion, was initially unavailable for comment. When approached by reporters, he quickly gained favor with the press corps by inviting them all to the bar provided that somebody could tell him where it was. There, he regaled the gathering with stories about unsightly skin conditions and sang a song about "a rather saucy goat."

The medal was to have been presented, as is traditional, by the chairman of the Norwegian Nobel Committee, Francis Sejedrsted, but a last-minute substitution had to be made when both Pirate Guys said they were uncomfortable with "a dude named Francis." Former Harlem Globetrotter Meadowlark Lemon was pressed into service, and later entertained the crowd by pretending to throw a bucket of water on Norway's King Harald, who had the basketball player shot.

Baur gave the acceptance speech for the pair as his inebriated partner stood upstage and played air guitar. Summers later led the audience in the wave, which was difficult for the mostly older crowd, which included an unusually high number of artificial hips.

While Peace Prize speeches usually run approximately an hour and a half, Baur and Summers clocked in at a tidy four minutes, thirteen seconds, and would easily have broken the four-minute mark had Baur not accidentally set fire to his note cards while lighting a cigarette during the presentation.

The speech went as follows:

"Thanks, Dave! And thank you, members of the committee and nations of the world, for believing in a dream. For actually dreaming that same dream and for making that dream, so absolutely dreamy. "What was that dream?" you may ask. Well sirs, and madams, and people whose gender is indeterminate, but still, you are people and we salute you, strange, non-sexed people. That dream was a world where, for just one shining moment ... well, 86,400 shining moments to be precise if we are considering each second in the day a 'moment' and that one DAY consisting of 86,400 moments being September 19th. Ah! I see the band leader is trying to hurry me up. You just settle down, there, Mr. Bandleader ... what? ... Oh, sorry Your Excellency. It appears our 'Mr. Bandleader' thinks he's the French Ambassador."

At this point, the respected American actor James Earl Jones, who had earlier given a stirring reading of the Dr. Martin Luther King, Jr. "I have a Dream" speech, stepped to the podium and whispered in Baur's ear.

"Is he really?" Baur asked. Jones nodded, and Baur hastily said, "I do apologize, Mr. Ambassador ... I mean, Mssr. Ambassadoerrrrr."

Summers stopped playing air guitar long enough to join his friend and co-founder at the podium and, making a hand sign he later called, "Satan's got your nose!" shouted, "AC/DC ROCKS!" This brought cheers from the Scottish delegation. Seeing the approval, he shouted toward the Canadian delegation, "Paul Shaffer ROCKS!" A similar response resounded through the hall. Caught up in the moment, the Swedish delegation leaped up and shouted, "ABBA ROCKS!" Summers' large face was pinched in what could only be described as a grimace, but before he could respond, Baur covered his mouth and turned smiling toward the crowd. "Yes," he said solemnly and with great earnestness, "Yes. ABBA DOES rock." The gathering of royalty, heads of state, diplomats, artists and modern philosophers cheered and hugged and wept, then broke into the chorus of "Dancing Queen." It appeared to this observer that Summers looked crossly at Baur and seemed to say only, "Dude" although he may have been saying "Jude" or possibly "food."

During the "after party" a clearly intoxicated Summers told the delegates how much he loved them and wanted to come visit them as soon as he could but couldn't understand why they got a "Noble Peach Prize." Baur regaled the journalists with a dramatic recitation of "The Cremation of Sam McGee." James Earl Jones put his arm around Dave Barry and said, "Those kids..." to which Barry responded, "Could you introduce me to them?"

Acknowledgments

Any pirate worth his salt knows the most important thing is a good crew. The Pirate Guys have been fortunate to have a better crew than they deserve. At the risk of forgetting someone, we'd like to specifically thank a few of you for all your help because you deserve it and in the hopes that you'll all definitely want to buy this book because your name is in it. And you'll probably want to buy copies for your friends and family as well.

First, to the women of Team Pirate – Tori Baur, the Official Lusty Pirate Wench, and Pat Kight, the Web Wench. Mark and John had lots of funny ideas. Tori and Pat did most of the heavy lifting. And to Wench In Waiting Toni Kight – Thanks for the ribs, Toni!

To Bennett Hall, who took on the courageous task of editing. Any mistakes that remain are our fault, not his. To Dr. Tom Costello and the folks at Word Association, thanks for bringing her home. For Don Maitz, the incredibly talented artist whose painting adorns this cover, you deserve a better vehicle than our effort.

To Rhonda Summers, for being a good sport.

To Cap'n Slappy's Pirate Players, Jan, Kris, Leonora, Anya, Pat, Janet, Dean, Mirinda, Alex, Erin and Paul; and all the good folks at ACT, especially Alan Nessett, Jan and Jim Donnelly and Reid and Angela Byers.

To our UK buddy, David Lindley (a mild-mannered British civil servant who sits down at the keyboard and becomes Sir Nigel de Pomfrit Coeur de Noir, the Scourge of the Seas.)

To Gary Tharp, Brian Rhodes, Sandy "Cementhands" McCormack, Gregg "Sawbones" Burgess, Grace Sanders,

Karen Watts, Christine "Jamaica Rose" Lampe and Tom Smith. Very special thanks to Jeff Boatwright and Gene and Susan Gregg – thanks for the beer.

Thanks to George Lauris and his improv class at LBCC, Barb Platt, Christi Sears, Robyn Olson, Keith Scribner, Scott Hoffman, Mark Jensen of the Seattle SeaFair Pirates, Sandi Wilson, Sarah Healy at Harcourt Childrens Books and CNN's Jeannie Moos.

To all the radio DJs and newspaper reporters around the world who got into the spirit and spread the word.

To all our friends at Albany Civic Theater, who were delighted for our success even as they were bemused by us.

Most especially, to our close personal friend, Pulitzer Prize-winner Dave Barry, and to his research department, Judi Smith, whose friendship we treasure, or at least covet.

And, finally, to Hasso Hering; it wouldn't have been as fun without your inspiration.